Marriage and Cohabitation

ISSUES

17
14 N
-7
-7

Volume 166

Series Editor

Lisa Firth

Independence
Educational Publishers
Cambridge

First published by Independence
The Studio, High Green
Great Shelford
Cambridge CB22 5EG
England

© Independence 2009

British Library Cataloguing in Publication Data
Marriage and Cohabitation – (Issues Series)
I. Marriage II. Family III. Unmarried couples IV. Firth, Lisa
306.8'1

ISBN 978 1 86168 470 7

Printed in Great Britain
MWL Print Group Ltd

Cover
The illustration on the front cover is by
Angelo Madrid.

CONTENTS

Useful information for readers

Dear Reader,

Issues: Marriage and Cohabitation

Is marriage in decline? Does it have any benefits over cohabitation? What does marriage mean to couples today? How are children affected by their parents divorcing, separating or remarrying? This title examines the issues surrounding marriage, divorce and the changing structure of the family. Chapters cover marriage trends and divorce and separation.

The purpose of Issues

Marriage and Cohabitation is the one hundred and sixty-sixth volume in the **Issues** series. The aim of this series is to offer up-to-date information about important issues in our world. Whether you are a regular reader or new to the series, we do hope you find this book a useful overview of the many and complex issues involved in the topic. This title replaces an older volume in the **Issues** series, Volume 106: **Trends in Marriage,** which is now out of print.

Titles in the **Issues** series are resource books designed to be of especial use to those undertaking project work or requiring an overview of facts, opinions and information on a particular subject, particularly as a prelude to undertaking their own research.

The information in this book is not from a single author, publication or organisation; the value of this unique series lies in the fact that it presents information from a wide variety of sources, including:

⇨ Government reports and statistics
⇨ Newspaper articles and features
⇨ Information from think-tanks and policy institutes
⇨ Magazine features and surveys
⇨ Website material
⇨ Literature from lobby groups and charitable organisations. *

Critical evaluation

Because the information reprinted here is from a number of different sources, readers should bear in mind the origin of the text and whether the source is likely to have a particular bias or agenda when presenting information (just as they would if undertaking their own research). It is hoped that, as you read about the many aspects of the issues explored in this book, you will critically evaluate the information presented. It is important that you decide whether you are being presented with facts or opinions. Does the writer give a biased or an unbiased report? If an opinion is being expressed, do you agree with the writer?

Marriage and Cohabitation offers a useful starting point for those who need convenient access to information about the many issues involved. However, it is only a starting point. Following each article is a URL to the relevant organisation's website, which you may wish to visit for further information.

Kind regards,

Lisa Firth
Editor, **Issues** series

*Please note that Independence Publishers has no political affiliations or opinions on the topics covered in the **Issues** series, and any views quoted in this book are not necessarily those of the publisher or its staff.*

Changing marriage

Information from One Plus One, the UK's leading relationships research organisation

Changing views

Getting married is still popular in Britain, with most people marrying at some point in their lives. Choosing to share your life with a partner is still the most common lifestyle choice. 57% of British households consisted of a married or cohabiting heterosexual couple in 2006.[4] However, the social role and meaning of marriage has changed.

> **When presented with a range of lifestyles to choose from 68% of those questioned chose 'being married with children' as their preferred lifestyle**

The traditional view of marriage, as a gateway to adulthood and independence, has become less common over the last generation. A One Plus One study[7] of marriage in the early 1980s showed that the attractiveness of marriage lay partly in the fact that it provided a 'package of rights', guaranteeing transition to adulthood. Today, it is more socially acceptable for couples to begin a sexual relationship, set up home and have children outside formal marriage. Young people no longer expect to get married and settle down as a matter of course.

People's views are changing largely because our views and ideals are shaped by the social climate within which we have grown up.

There are dramatic differences between the views of those aged 55 and above and younger people. The most notable shifts in attitudes are among 35- to 54-year-olds, this group are more likely to have cohabited than their parents' generation for example.[2]

Traditional views are more likely to be held by religious and married people. Differences in educational background also point to differences in attitudes. Those without qualifications hold more traditional views than those with higher educational qualifications. However, among those people with educational qualifications those with higher or more advanced qualifications are more traditional in their outlook than those with lower qualifications.[2]

Emerging patterns

Between 1984 and 2006, the proportion of people thinking there is 'rarely or nothing wrong at all' with pre-marital sex increased from 48% to 70%,[4] while the proportion thinking it to be always wrong decreased from 15% to 6%.[4] It is also increasingly uncommon for first sexual intercourse to take place within marriage. In 2006, it was found that 36%[1] of the British population have been in a cohabiting relationship at some point and that 11%[1] of the population were currently in a cohabiting relationship. Many cohabiting relationships will turn into marriages with 56%[1] ending in marriage rather than breaking up.

73% of people aged under 35 and living in with a partner expect to marry each other whilst only about one in eight never expect to marry.[5]

85% of people aged 65 or above think that marriage and parenthood should go hand in hand, compared with just over a third of 18- to 24-year-olds.[2] However, even among the most traditional groups (for example older or religious people), views about the relationship between marriage and parenthood have changed.[2]

In 1989, almost 75% of the population believed that 'people who want children ought to get married'. Five years later, in 1994, this had fallen to 57%; in 2000, just over half the population subscribed to this view.[5] In 2006, just over 44% of births were outside marriage, more than four times the proportion in 1975.[10]

Marriage as the ideal

One survey[9] shows that, when presented with a range of lifestyles to choose from, 68% of those questioned chose 'being married with children' as their preferred lifestyle, and 77% disagreed with the statement 'marriage is dead'.

Young people also reaffirm the symbolic significance of marriage. A survey[16] exploring young people's lives in Britain found that only 4%

of young people agreed with the statement 'Marriage is old-fashioned and no longer relevant' and 89% said that they would like to get married at some time in the future.

However, findings from the British Social Attitudes Survey suggest that, whilst marriage is still widely valued as an ideal, it is regarded with much more ambivalence in terms of everyday partnering and parenting.

Only 4% of young people agreed with the statement 'Marriage is old-fashioned and no longer relevant' and 89% said that they would like to get married at some time in the future

---

Analysis of marriage expectations suggests that cohabiting partners are less likely to marry each other once they have had a baby: a larger proportion of women with children than childless women (60% compared with 45%) never wish to marry their present partner, and the results are similar for men (66% compared with 47%)[5].

Ermisch (2000)[5] suggests that this may partly be explained by the uncertainty some couples have about committing to each other. Partners unsure about marrying each other are more likely to have a child in a cohabiting union, while cohabiting couples who plan to marry, marry first and then have children. A study by Stanley, Markman and Rhoades[14] found that those cohabitants who planned to marry were happier in their relationships than those who did not make plans to marry. And that those who drifted into marriage through force of habit or for financial reasons were more likely to experience relationship distress later in their relationship.

Further analysis of marriage expectations suggests that 15-20% of never married, childless people aged between 16 and 35 do not expect to marry at all[5].

Changing emphases: 'Institutional v Relational'
Romantic love is usually portrayed in our culture as the single most important motive for marriage. Nevertheless, research by One Plus One[7] has found that many factors inspire newlyweds to marry – a gradual feeling of disillusionment about being single, fears of growing old alone, as well as a feeling that they were now ready for marriage.

Morgan (1992)[8], along with other commentators, sees the nature of marriage as moving from an institutional to a relational (meaning relationships based on love and companionship) model. Burgess and Locke (1945)[3] describe how, in the past, the unity of family life was shaped in relation to the formal authority of the law, tradition, public opinion and ritual, and rigid disciplinary systems.

In contrast, the emergence of a new family form – the companionate family – regards personal relations between partners as the key element of family life. Stone (1979)[15] discusses how an early rise in relational/companionate marriage began in the 18th century (particularly among the upper and middle classes), when future spouses started to have more freedom to choose marriage partners for themselves.

Many of these young people put the prospect of emotional satisfaction before the ambition for increased income or status. This, in turn, helped to equalise relationships between husband and wife. Partners began to address each other in more affectionate terms and were more likely than before to set up home on their own away from their families. A honeymoon period during which the young couple were left alone to get to know each other sexually and emotionally became an accepted ritual.

Whilst the value attached to equality and sharing in modern marriage has certainly increased in the last 50 years, behaviour within marriage is still highly influenced by the institutional model of marriage. In particular, the reality of married life continues to be one of relative inequality around domestic duties.

Although women's participation in paid work has greatly increased during the 20th century, this has not been matched by an equivalent increase in men's participation in household and caring work[6]. Men have been slower to respond to the changes in women's attitudes and practices.

It is important to bear in mind that the 'institutional' and 'relational' models of marriage are ideal types: modern marriages usually contain elements of both. Economics, for example, play an important part in the process and negotiations of

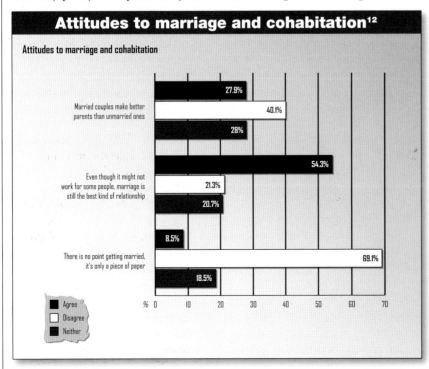

Attitudes to marriage and cohabitation[12]

Attitudes to marriage and cohabitation

Married couples make better parents than unmarried ones: 27.9%, 40.1%, 28%

Even though it might not work for some people, marriage is still the best kind of relationship: 54.3%, 21.3%, 20.7%

There is no point getting married, it's only a piece of paper: 8.5%, 69.1%, 18.5%

Agree / Disagree / Neither

married life, if not in the initial choice of partner.

Similarly, historians and family researchers express scepticism about whether modern marital relationships are inspired entirely by private romantic ideals. Expensive and elaborate weddings have become popular. To many the wedding represents the private couple making a public commitment – combining both the relational and institutional elements of marriage. According to a recent online poll, couples now spend an average of just over £20,000 on their wedding[18].

45% of marriages will have ended in divorce before the couple reach their diamond wedding anniversary

Over the life cycle of a marriage, relational or institutional elements are likely to predominate at different times. In the early years, when romantic love is at its peak, the relational form may be more pronounced. After the arrival of children, marriages usually undergo changes which more accurately reflect institutional marriage. Domestic chores become increasingly segregated along gender lines, wider family such as grandparents become involved in the young family's life, and the presence of children means that the State starts to take more interest in the private world of the couple.

After children leave home the marriage may move back to a more companionate form, with the couple devoting more time to each other – as people live longer now this period can last up to 30 years.

His or her marriage?

Married women talk about 'togetherness' in marriage and sharing a 'common life' with their husbands (meaning sharing interests and time with their partner). Men, on the other hand, maintain a concept of togetherness that contains elements

of traditional marriage. Men are more likely to emphasise the importance of knowing that a wife can be a source of support if necessary and are less likely to stress the need to have time for talking together. Young husbands' views of togetherness have more to do with geographical closeness than emotional closeness (Mansfield and Collard, 1988)[7].

It is possible that the women's movement has been an important catalyst in the progress towards an increasingly strong emphasis on equality and sharing in marriage. Women seem to have moved towards the relational model of marriage earlier and faster than men.

Ending marriage and relationships

In a 2008[17] study of relationship dissolution, it was found that 45% of marriages will have ended in divorce before the couple reach their diamond (60th) wedding anniversary. Another 45% will have ended due to the death of one partner and 10% will be intact. Although the divorce rate is falling this is reflected in the marriage statistics. The divorce rate is linked to the proportion of the population who are married. If there are fewer people in the pool of married people then proportionately there are fewer divorces.

The Divorce Reform Act in England and Wales came into effect in 1971. This made seeking a divorce easier and the number of divorces increased, peaking in 1993[11].

Attitudes towards divorce have changed over time. In 2006, 63% of people thought that 'divorce can be a positive step towards a new life' and

78% agreed that 'it is not divorce that harms children, but conflict between their parents'[4]. It is important to remember however, that despite falling divorce rates this does not mean people aren't experiencing relationship distress. Today more and more people cohabit and choose a variety of relationship lifestyles. Although the statistics show a drop in the numbers of those divorcing, this does not mean that any fewer relationships are really coming to an end.

References

1 Barlow, A., Burgoyne, C., Clery, E. & Smithson, J. (2008). Cohabitation and the law: myths, money and the media. In A. Park, J. Curtice, K. Thomson, M. Phillips, M. Johnson & E. Clery (Eds.) British Social Attitudes: The 24th Report (pp.29-51). London: Sage.

2 Barlow, A., Duncan, S., James, G. & Park, A. (2001). Just a piece of paper? Marriage and cohabitation. In A. Park, J. Curtice, K. Thomson, L. Jarvis & C. Bromley (Eds). British Social Attitudes: Public Policy, Social Ties: The 18th Report (pp.29-57). London: Sage.

3 Burgess, E.W. & Locke, H.J. (1945). The family: from institution to companionship. New York: American Book Publishers.

4 Duncan , S. & Phillips, M. (2008). New families? Tradition and change in modern relationships. In A. Park, J. Curtice, K. Thomson, M. Phillips, M. Johnson & E. Clery (Eds.). British Social Attitudes: The 24th Report (pp.1-28). London: Sage.

5 Ermisch, JF. (2000). Personal Relationships and Marriage Expectations: Evidence from the 1998 British

Two models of marriage[13]

Institution	Relationship
- Less freedom of choice of marriage partners	- Greater freedom of choice
- Marriage linked to wider societal and/or kinship obligations	- Marriage relatively separate from wider social and/or kinship obligations
- Emphasis upon economic aspects of marriage e.g. property and the sexual division of labour	- Emphasis upon the emotional and personal aspects of marriage
- Public emphasis	- Private emphasis
- Marriage as one of a set of social relationships	- Marriage as the central relationship
- Relative inequality within marriage	- Relative equality within marriage; companionship
- Little emphasis on mutual sexuality; sexuality linked to procreation	- Positive emphasis on sexuality; sexual dysfunction seen as sign of marital problems

Household Panel study. Essex: Institute for Social and Economic Research.

6 Gershuny, J., Godwin, M. & Jones, S. (1994) The domestic labour revolution: a process of lagged adaptation. In M. Anderson, F. Bechhofer, J. Gershuny (Eds.) *The social and political economy of the household.* Oxford: Oxford University Press.

7 Mansfield, P. & Collard, J. (1988). *The beginning of the rest of your life?* Basingstoke: MacMillan.

8 Morgan, D. (1992). Marriage and society: understanding an era of change. In J. Lewis, D. Clark, D. Morgan (Eds.).*Whom God hath joined together.* London: Routledge.

9 MORI Polls and Surveys (1999). *Family and Marriage Poll.* London: MORI Corporate Communications.

10 National Statistics (2007). *Birth Statistics: Review of the Registrar General on Birth Patterns of Family Building in England and Wales,* 2006. Series FM1, no 38. London: HMSO.

11 National Statistics (2008). *Social Trends 38.* Hampshire: Palgrave MacMillan.

12 Park, A., Curtice, J., Thomson, K., Phillips, M., Johnson, M. & Clery, E. (2008). *British Social Attitudes: The 24th Report.* Appendix III. London: Sage.

13 Reynolds, J. & Mansfield, P. (1999) The effect of changing attitudes to marriage on its stability. In *High divorce rates: The state of the evidence on reasons and remedies.* Vol 1. 1999. London: The Lord Chancellor's Department Research Secretariat.

14 Stanley, SC., Rhoades, GK. & Markman, HJ. (2006) *Sliding versus deciding: Inertia and premarital cohabitation effect.* Family Relations, 55 (October), 499-509.

15 Stone, L. (1979). *The family, sex and marriage in England 1500-1800.* Harmondsworth: Penguin.

16 The Opinion Research Business (2000). *Young People's Lives in Britain Today.* London: The Opinion Research Business.

17 Wilson, B. & Smallwood, S. (2008). The proportion of marriages ending in divorce. *Population Trends,* 131 (Spring), 28-36.

18 You & Your Wedding, (2008). *Is your wedding average?* [online]. Available from: http://www. youandyourwedding.co.uk/ index.php/v1/Is_your_wedding_ average%3F [Accessed Oct 2008].

Updated October 2008

⇨ The above information is reprinted with kind permission from One Plus One. Visit www.oneplusone. org.uk for more information.

Marriage, relationships and family trends

Parents' relationship with each other affects their children's wellbeing. Does the state have any power to influence this, and should it?

Key statistics

⇨ In 2006 there were 236,980 weddings in England and Wales, of which 39 per cent were remarriages for one or both parties.[1]

⇨ There were 132,562 divorces in England and Wales in 2006, the lowest divorce rate since 1984.[2]

⇨ While marriage rates have fallen steadily since the early 1970s when there were over 450,000 a year, divorce rates have remained relatively constant over the same period.[3]

⇨ In 1971 the mean age of men and women at first marriage was 24 and 22 respectively. By 2004, it was 31 for men and 29 for women.[4]

⇨ In 2006 23 per cent of children in Great Britain were living in lone-parent families. This has increased from 21 per cent in 1997 and 7 per cent in 1972.[5]

⇨ 37 per cent of children of lone parents live in poverty in the UK (under 60 per cent of median household income before housing costs) compared to 18 per cent of children in couple families.[6]

⇨ In 2006, 56% of births in the UK were to married couples.[7] The majority of the remainder were to cohabiting parents (estimated three-fifths in England and Wales, 2005).[8]

More support is needed for couples to build strong, resilient relationships, including support for parents and children during and after relationship breakdown

⇨ Divorce and separation can increase the chances of poor

outcomes for children. However, these are not inevitable. The likelihood of poor outcomes is increased by financial hardship; family conflict before, during and after separation; and multiple changes in family structure. Quality contact with the non-resident parent can improve outcomes.[9]

In 2006 there were 236,980 weddings in England and Wales, of which 39 per cent were remarriages for one or both parties

---

⇨ It is not just parental separation that has an impact on children: the quality of their parents' relationship also affects their wellbeing. In research commissioned by FPI, seven out of ten young people, in contrast to only a third of adults, said that it was important that parents should get on well together in order to raise happy children.[10]

⇨ Both prevention and crisis intervention are needed, starting in schools with a focus on relationships as well as biological sex education. Relationship support and advice should be easily available from magazines, helplines, health visitors, schools and family workers. Support for parents and children before, during and after separation needs to be dramatically improved, with a focus on child-inclusive mediation.

Financial incentives for married couples would be counter-productive

⇨ Benefits to married couples at the expense of others are a risky strategy. In the short term they will penalise children who are already worse off, in the hope of influencing behaviour to create more stable relationships in the long term. This is doubtful because:

↳ The financial incentive would be small compared to the difference between maintaining a household with one adult or with two.

↳ Even supposing that they did encourage cohabiting couples to marry for financial reasons, it is not known to what extent the marriage bond creates relationship stability as opposed to more stable couples choosing to marry.

The debate needs to be shifted from moral panic about a decline of the nuclear family and a rise in single parents, towards evidence-based policy

⇨ Sweden, Denmark and Norway, ranked highest in the 2007 UNICEF report on child well-being, have similar proportions of children in lone-parent families to the UK, but a much lower child poverty rate.[11] These countries are notable for their high quality childcare and are much more equal societies than the UK.

⇨ In 2005, more than 10 per cent of all families with dependent children in Great Britain were stepfamilies.[12]

⇨ These families face particular challenges which should be recognised in Government policy.

References

1 Office for National Statistics (2008) Marriages: 4% fall in UK marriages. Online at: http://www.statistics.gov.uk/cci/nugget.asp?id=322

2 Office for National Statistics (2008) Divorces: Divorces fall by 7% in 2006. Online at: http://www.statistics.gov.uk/cci/nugget.asp?id=170

3 Office for National Statistics (2007) *Social Trends*. Palgrave Macmillan

4 Office for National Statistics (2008) *Social Trends*. Palgrave Macmillan

5 Office for National Statistics (2007) *Social Trends*. Palgrave Macmillan

6 Department for Work and Pensions (2008) *Households Below Average Income (HBAI) 1994/95-2006/07*. Department for Work and Pensions

7 Office for National Statistics (2008) *Social Trends*. Palgrave Macmillan

8 Office for National Statistics (2007) *Social Trends*. Palgrave Macmillan

9 Rodgers, B. and Pryor, J. (1998) *Divorce and separation: the outcomes for children*. Joseph Rowntree Foundation.

10 National Family and Parenting Institute (2000) *Teenagers' attitudes to parenting: A survey of young people's experiences of being parented, and their views on how to bring up children*. Survey conducted by MORI

11 UNICEF (2007) *Child Poverty in Perspective: An Overview of Child Well-being in Rich Countries*. Innocenti Report Card 7. Unicef

12 Office for National Statistics (2007) *Social Trends*. Palgrave Macmillan

Are we witnessing the demise of the traditional nuclear family structure?

By Claire James, Family and Parenting Institute
Updated June 2008

⇨ The above information is reprinted with kind permission from the Family and Parenting Institute. Visit www.familyandparenting.org for more information.

Marriage rates fall to lowest on record

Information from the Office for National Statistics

Marriage rates in England and Wales have fallen to the lowest level since records began, according to provisional figures for 2006 released today by the Office for National Statistics.

The number of unmarried adults rose in 2006, but the number who chose to marry fell, producing the lowest marriage rates since they were first calculated in 1862. In 2006 the marriage rate for men was 22.8 men marrying per 1,000 unmarried men aged 16 and over, down from 24.5 in 2005. The marriage rate for women in 2006 was 20.5 women marrying per 1,000 unmarried women aged 16 and over, down from 21.9 in 2005.

The number of marriages fell by 4 per cent in 2006 compared with 2005 to 236,980. With the exception of an increase between 2002 and 2004, this follows the declining long-term trend observed in recent decades and is the lowest annual number of marriages since 1895 when there were 228,204.

Marriages that were the first for both parties in 2006 accounted for 61 per cent of all marriages and remarriages for both parties accounted for 18 per cent. These proportions are similar to those observed in 2005. Since 1981, marriages that were the first for both parties have fallen by 37 per cent, while remarriages have fallen by a quarter.

Other statistics for 2006 show that:
⇨ Since 1991, the average age at marriage has increased by just less than five years for men and just over four and a half years for women. In 2006 the mean age at marriage for all marriages increased to 36.4 years for men and 33.7 years for women, compared with 2005 when the figures were 36.2 and 33.5 respectively. In 2006 the mean age at first marriage was 31.8 years for men and 29.7 years for women.
⇨ The number of civil marriage ceremonies fell 3 per cent from 2005, from 162,169 to 157,490. Civil ceremonies represented 66 per cent of all ceremonies in 2006, up from 65 per cent in 2005. In 1990 this figure was 47 per cent.
⇨ The number of religious ceremonies fell by 7 per cent to 79,490 compared with 2005. Since 1991 this figure has halved compared with a fall in the number of all marriages of 23 per cent in the same period. Religious ceremonies accounted for 34 per cent of all marriages in 2006.
⇨ The number of ceremonies taking place in approved premises has continued to increase. Just over 95,300 marriages took place in approved premises in 2006 accounting for 40 per cent of all marriages and 60 per cent of civil marriages. In 2005, 36 per cent of marriages took place in approved premises; in 1996 this proportion was 5 per cent.

Final figures for 2005 released today show that marriages fell by 9 per cent across England and Wales compared with 2004. A fall was experienced in all Government Office Regions in England and in Wales. The largest fall occurred in London (29 per cent) and the smallest was observed in the North East (3 per cent).

There was a change in law from 1 February 2005, which was designed to discourage 'sham marriages'. This is one of many factors that may have contributed to the fall in the number of marriages in 2006 and 2005.

Final figures for divorces in 2005 were also released today. These statistics show that divorces rates fell in 2005 compared with 2004 to 13.1 divorces per 1,000 married people in England and Wales and the number of divorces fell by 8 per cent compared with the previous year.
26 March 2008

⇨ The above information is reprinted with kind permission from the Office for National Statistics. Visit www.statistics.gov.uk for more information.

© Crown copyright

Cohabitees aspire towards marriage

Marriage still the ideal for many couples currently living together

Despite rising levels of cohabitation in Britain, marriage still remains the ideal for many couples, finds new research by Dr Ernestina Coast, lecturer in Population Studies in the Social Policy Department at LSE.

> When questioned about their future intentions, three-quarters of men and women reported that they were planning to, or probably would, get married

The study, *Honourable Intentions? Attitudes and Intentions among Currently Cohabiting Couples in Britain*, was presented at the British Society for Population Studies in 2007 and the European Association for Population Studies in 2008.

Dr Coast analysed BHPS data on the marriage expectations and reasons for cohabiting from people aged under 35 who have never been married and are currently in cohabiting relationships. Her findings included:

⇨ Two-thirds of men and women report that there is no positive advantage in living as a couple rather than being married.

⇨ Childless men and women are significantly more likely to report that there are advantages in living together as a couple rather than being married.

⇨ When questioned about the reasons for viewing cohabitation as being advantageous compared with marriage, mothers are significantly more likely to report financial advantages compared with fathers.

⇨ Childless women are significantly more likely to see cohabitation as a 'trial marriage' compared with cohabiting women who are already mothers.

⇨ When questioned about their future intentions, three-quarters of men and women reported that they were planning to, or probably would, get married.

Across Europe, the proportion of never-married individuals who are in cohabiting relationships is rising. According to the Government Actuary's Department, by 2031 more than 30 per cent of never-married people aged 18-59 are projected to be in cohabiting relationships in Britain. *6 July 2007*

⇨ The above information is reprinted with kind permission from the London School of Economics and Political Science. Visit www.lse.ac.uk for more information.

© London School of Economics and Political Science

Marriage survey results

Information from Seddons

Million of Brits are stuck in unhappy marriages but will not walk away for fear of financial or emotional hardship, a report revealed yesterday. The study revealed 59 per cent of women would end their marriage today if their future financial security was assured.

Meanwhile 51 per cent of men said they were in a 'loveless' marriage.

It also emerged that 13 per cent of women and 10 per cent of men wished they'd married someone else. Yesterday a Relate spokesperson said: 'It's so easy for married couples to get stuck in a rut once the realities of paying the bills and getting the children's breakfast sets in.

> 51 per cent of men said they were in a 'loveless' marriage

'Relationships inevitably change over time. Couples who address their problems and talk to each other when they feel they may be taken for granted, stand a better chance of pulling through.

'Divorce impacts on every single area of a person's life. Dividing up the family home, pets and everything they own together is just part of the process.'

The survey was commissioned by top London solicitors Seddons in the wake of a rush of divorce applications in the first week of the New Year. Twelve per cent of couples said they are in a loveless relationship and over a third (35 per cent) believe their marriage will turn stale in the near future.

A massive 29 per cent said they were staying in a doomed marriage to save themselves going through a massive upheaval – and 37 per cent said they were staying for the sake of the children

A staggering 56 per cent of people admitted they weren't completely happy in their relationship – and more than half said they had considered splitting from their partner. The poll, of 2,000 married Brits, also revealed that 12 per cent would stay in an unhappy relationship just for an easy life. One in five quizzed said they wished to split from the person they're with but are kept from doing so.

A massive 29 per cent said they were staying in a doomed marriage to save themselves going through a massive upheaval – and 37 per cent said they were staying for the sake of the children. Some are worried about what they would lose if they left their partner, with 42 per cent fearing they would have to give up their home if they split.

Almost a third of those surveyed are worried they would be left with absolutely nothing if they walked out on their marriage. And 30 per cent of men are scared that they would have to leave without their children. More than half also admit they would miss the financial security that comes from being with their partner. But nearly half of those polled would stay with their partner for the sake of the family unit.

Deborah Jeff, from Seddons Solicitors which carried out the poll, said: 'One in three marriages ends in divorce but only one in five use mediation.

'Worryingly, some 60 per cent of people in the survey were not aware of how mediation can be used to improve communication between the parties, minimise the impact of divorce and keep legal fees to a minimum.

'This means that many couples will spend too much money on lawyers' fees and many may end up with less than ideal contact arrangements – which can be disastrous for parents and children alike.

'It is also important for separating couples to consider how mediation after financial disclosure may result in a quicker financial settlement, again keeping costs to a minimum and reducing acrimony in those discussions.'

Half of Brits would consider going to see a counsellor in an attempt to get their relationship back on track before heading for the divorce courts.

However, one in five don't reckon it would be worth the hassle.

For a quarter of Brits quizzed, the thought of high legal fees prevents them from having a divorce and six out of 10 haven't heard of mediation for divorce settlements.

17 January 2008

⇨ The above information is reprinted with kind permission from Seddons, the international law firm. Visit www.seddons.co.uk for more information.

© Seddons

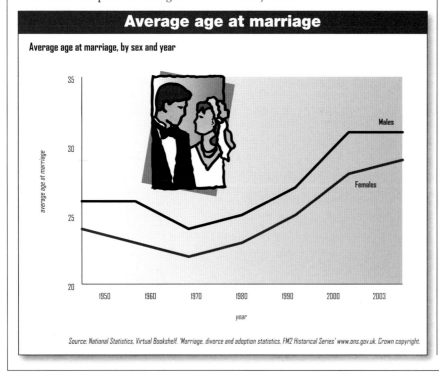

Average age at marriage

Average age at marriage, by sex and year

Source: National Statistics, Virtual Bookshelf. 'Marriage, divorce and adoption statistics, FM2 Historical Series' www.ons.gov.uk. Crown copyright.

Is it the beginning of the end for marriage?

Hannah Betts reveals why she is part of the new generation who will never tie the knot

The bouquet curves towards me in a hideous slow-motion arc. I back away from the throng of scrambling womanhood, but, nightmarishly, the more I endeavour to elude this marital missile the closer it looms, until it hits me square on the head, sliding down my body to rest at my feet. Appalled, I shudder backwards, arms planted at my sides. A stunned silence prevails as the entire wedding party regards me with clinical fascination. Finally the chief bridesmaid tuts, bends forward, scoops up and dusts down the bouquet, before brandishing it half-heartedly in the air.

Platitude has it that it is every little girl's dream to be metamorphosed into a billowing white cloud. I was no exception, only mine was a recurrent, Angela Carter-esque nightmare: my dress a shroud, the groom a vampire, my train snaked around my throat removing first speech then vital signs.

In adult life the dreams prove still more tormenting. My refusal to marry has been the cause of painful separations (I now no longer sleep with advocates of the institution, although nothing propels a chap to seek to knot-tie more than a partner disinclined). My refusenik stance is the cause of baffled offence from friends, followed by aggressively emotional attempts at conversion. It is a constant provocation to colleagues, with the result that I find myself editing wedding sections (the ignominy!), or being dispatched to road-test designer wedding dresses (my body rebelled, generating my first freak period in 25 years, an occurrence that did not sit happily amid £12,000 of tulle). When my sister announced her engagement I was appalled that someone I thought I knew could do something so alien,

psychologically dubious, banal. While she, quite rightly, felt that a simple 'Congratulations' would have sufficed.

Gamophobia – fear of marriage – is a little-used term to mark a still less acknowledged concept. I hold my hands up to it, not waving but drowning under the rampant gamomania of society at large, where £20,000 is the average nuptial spend and nothing blinds like the glare of a white frock. I am wedding-phobic, but no less averse to the institution itself. According to my own peculiarly fundamentalist secular beliefs marriage is lazy, anachronistic, morally bankrupt. Moreover, in the same way that if there were a God, He is not one I'd wish to have any truck with, so if marriage were the only thing holding a union of mine together, then I'd rather let it pass. (Hence the bumper-sticker axiom that abstainers 'get to choose their partner every day'.)

There are many things that my objection does not entail: fear of commitment (nope); a reflection on my parents' relationship (they are still together); a judgement as to whether or not I want children (neither here nor there); and that great patronising lie that I am yet to meet 'the right man'. Nor am I some joyless ideologue – I'm rather in favour of a good knees up, and have no objection whatsoever to being presented with jewellery.

Forced to unpack my antipathy, I would cite four po-faced motives: atheism; feminism; a loathing of state and/or public intervention in matters I deem private; and something more oddball regarding the close-down of narrative possibility. One reason would be enough to quash any Doris Day ambition; the four together topple into each other like spinsterish dominoes.

My stance may be at the more neurotic, proposing-as-a-dumping-offence extreme, but I am by no means alone in my disinclination towards getting hitched. Rates of marriage in Britain – 283,730 in 2005 – are at their lowest since 1896. Given the ebb and flow of population, this is the most paltry scoring since records began almost 150 years ago. Divorce statistics may have fallen (there being fewer candidates), yet, still, 40 per cent of first marriages and 70 per cent of second shots end in divorce.

'My life with my partner is a private seal of my commitment to her. We don't need our status authenticated by institutions outside our own personal one'

The attitudes reflected in these statistics suggest that love and marriage do indeed go together like a horse and carriage in the sense that both are quaint anachronisms. According to this year's British Social Attitudes (BSA) Survey, published in January, two-thirds of people see little difference between marriage and cohabitation (a mere one-fifth taking issue). Even regarding children, where more traditional views tend to apply, only one in four people believes that married couples make better parents. Meanwhile, over half declare weddings to be more about celebration than lifelong commitment, with two-thirds endorsing the truism that divorce can be 'a positive step towards a new life'. As Professor Simon Duncan, co-author of the marriage chapter, decreed: 'The heterosexual married couple is no longer central as a social norm.'

Indeed, the heterosexual married couple shows every sign of taking its role model from *Who's Afraid of Virginia Woolf?* In a survey released in the wake of the annual post-Christmas divorce rush, over half of 2,000 adults confessed to being unhappy in their marriage. A staggering two-thirds of wives revealed that they would divorce immediately were their economic security assured. A plaintive half of husbands considered their marriages loveless, while 30 per cent of those questioned were lingering in doomed marriages 'to avoid upheaval'.

Experts recommend caution in regarding the British public as increasingly wedlock-averse. According to Penny Mansfield, director of the relationship research organisation One Plus One, 'There is very little indication that people are opposed to marriage; simply evidence that people are not getting married. In the main, people don't see any difference between the institution and long-term cohabitation. Those in relationships who are not married simply see themselves as being just like people who are. People don't really think about it.'

The effect is a massive backing away from what, even in the reputedly swinging Sixties and Seventies, was a fundamental rite of passage for the vast majority. Whether its abstainers are actively resistant or merely nonchalant, what we are seeing is, if not the end of marriage, then quite possibly the beginning of the end. So who are these conjugal avoiders?

For some, refusal to marry is a God thing. Ryan Thompson, 28, a journalist for *Men's Health*, is adamant: 'I don't believe in marriage because I don't believe in God.' Like me, as a teenager, Thompson taunted his married parents for their ideological weakness; his views have also been the cause of relationship meltdown. 'If I were not so fundamentally against it, I'd probably have a nice legal bill now, less hair, and would never have met my current partner. Marriage has long been a publicly acknowledged contract of convenience. My life with my partner is a private seal of my

commitment to her. We don't need our status authenticated by institutions outside our own personal one.'

The feminist thing is no less compelling. Hailing from multicultural Birmingham, I did not attend a traditional Christian wedding until my mid-twenties. Words cannot express my head-spinning, *Carrie*-style horror at the revelation that my friend, a lawyer, was being walked down the aisle by one man to be handed over to another, a (rather less distinguished) lawyer whom she promised to obey, the whole thing rounded off by a series of male speeches while she remained silent in her faux virgin's white. Ten years on, another friend, the breadwinner in her relationship, was instructed by the officiating cleric to submit to her husband in all matters, to thunderous masculine applause.

Of course, a good many feminists put a less Stepford stamp on their ceremonies, and go on to draw great strength from their marriages, considering themselves to have reinvented its limits. Personally, I find this as impossible a notion as the idea that one could somehow reinvent slavery. Marriage is the sum of its history; a history that encompasses subordination, drudgery, property theft, and, well within my lifetime, the legal impossibility of rape. In this context, not only would I be mortified to participate in such a structure myself, I would be ashamed to bring

up children in such a shoddy and despicable arrangement.

Elizabeth Enright, 30, an Edinburgh psychologist, concurs: 'I certainly have feminist issues around the history of marriage as a tradition of buying and selling women. I can't believe other women are so unselfconscious about it, and surprised that I have a desire to be neither princess nor chattel.' Younger women are no less open to these qualms. Susie Corbett, a 21-year-old customer services employee from Sheffield, rejects the term feminist – 'as I think it connotes a scary, angry woman' – but her suspicion of marriage reveals no little feminist content. 'It's a dated concept. I don't believe that a wife should stay at home while the husband goes out to work. The roles of men and women have become more equal.'

Nadia Idle, 27, an anti-poverty campaigner from London, prefers to consider herself as 'radical independent left-wing' rather than feminist. 'My position on marriage stems from my political beliefs and my lack of religious affiliation. I don't need or want the approval of the state or any religious authority to enter into a relationship. I don't need an artificial contract to make me feel secure. Anthropologically, marriage fulfilled an important social function in organising society which I just don't think emancipated individuals need to adhere to.'

Underlying many such statements is a disapproval of state or even community investment in what is a private relationship. For many refuseniks, the very thing that draws others to marry – a declaration before family and friends – proves repellent. (I recall having to explain to a former partner that a party with speeches and fancy outfits in the orangery at Blenheim Palace would not really cut it as far as non-marriage went.)

The very notion still causes Caitlyn Jones, a 35-year-old charity worker from Bristol, discomfort. 'When I was about eight, one of the things I feared most about adulthood was marriage. I would lie in bed and worry about having to walk down an aisle and kiss a man in front of loads of people while wearing some hideous dress. The embarrassment factor was a huge turn-off, but the name-change even more so. I really couldn't get my head around the idea that a woman had to take a man's surname. As I got older it turned out that my suspicions were not unfounded. I've never been proposed to and I hope I never will.'

A few of us also wrestle with what might be categorised as marriage's shutdown of narrative possibility – not the possibility of further erotic adventure per se, but the possibility of adventure at large. Marriage is the end not the beginning of most women's stories; there will not be much to say after 'Reader, I married him.' As an adolescent, I was powerfully moved by the opening of D.H. Lawrence's *Women in Love*, with its heroines' assertion of their modernity by renouncing connubial ambition.

The writer and broadcaster Nadine Baggott, 45, expresses similar feelings: 'I have never wanted to get married, not for one second. I think it's because I watched too many Bette Davis and Joan Crawford films and identified with those wisecracking, fast-talking dames. If it were a case of choosing between being Doris Day and Joan Crawford, I would always choose to be the mistress, never the wife. The bride's story ended with marriage, because after the wedding there was never anything interesting worth filming. And so today, in essence, after years of living with my partner, I am a "wife" and we are "married",' she says, 'but I stick to the fact that I am still the girlfriend and we live together because for me being married means being boring and predictable and conforming to what is expected.'

For many, hostility to the state of wedlock will be the price of already having conformed. Richard Quick, 35, a London publisher, married at 26 and separated at 29, when his second child was two, the age he was when his own parents parted. 'I thought my parents' experience meant I was well-armed for marriage,' Quick says. 'In fact, I was just well-prepared for divorce.' Would he remarry? 'No, I just don't see any need. It's an outmoded institution. Children would be better served by broader, more open family units. In our modern consumer society we pick what we want from

any situation, but marriage is still one-size-fits-all. We need to unbundle those vows, to cherry-pick the bits we want. That way there'd be a lot less disappointment.'

Quick leaves potential partners in no doubt regarding his position. 'I've found it actually helps narrow the field. There was a time when saying that marriage was off the cards was as bad as saying you didn't want kids, but that's changed once women have got past their Barbie doll stage.'

Indeed, Dr Jane Lewis, Professor of Social Policy at the London School of Economics, argues that these days marriage involves no small degree of risk for women. 'At the beginning of the 20th century marriage offered protection of a sort. If the marriage worked, it was probably the best way of coping economically. Today, the costs of marriage in terms of childbearing are front-loaded for women. What if one marries, gives up work while the children are young, sacrificing pension contributions, earnings, promotion prospects – and then the husband leaves? Marriage has become a risk,' says Lewis. 'The more economic independence one has, the more one can protect against that risk.'

Professor Lewis agrees with Penny Mansfield that Britons are not necessarily turning away from wedlock so much as deferring it. 'It's just that people no longer operate according to the old rules ordering sex, children and marriage,' Lewis says.

Relate changed its name from the National Marriage Guidance Council 20 years ago to reflect this shifting demographic. Jenny North, Relate's head of public policy, has also observed a sea change whereby couples have come to regard marriage as the pinnacle not the premise of their relationship. 'In the past, marriage was something one did en route to adulthood. These days it often comes after one's got the house and the car, when the job is going well, when you've had the baby, as the sign to those around you that you've made it. People aspire to and idealise marriage, only wanting to do it when all the pieces have fallen into place and everything's perfect – and because of

this, marriage has become identified with the wedding.'

Perfection being the impossible dream it is, this results in couples indefinitely postponing their weddings. Lucy Wigmore, 32, lives in the Midlands and has two children. 'I strongly want my children to have married parents, but we just haven't got round to it. We're too busy to plan something and can't afford a big party right now. Plus I'd like to get my figure back. So we're looking at the end of 2009, later perhaps.'

There's no business like nuptial show business. As Penny Mansfield remarks: 'In Alan Bennett's *Untold Stories*, he recalls his parents getting married at 8am because they wanted to avoid the spotlight. But in our celebrity culture, everyone wants to show off.' This exhibitionism is one of the many aspects of knot-tying that repulses 36-year-old Southampton researcher Tom Richards. 'The spectacle involved in modern marriage is in inverse proportion to its meaning. The more devoid of content the institution becomes, the more a grotesquely postmodern, style-over-substance principle applies. The entire event becomes a swaggering parody of some bygone society wedding.'

⇨ This is an extract from an article published in *The Observer* on 2 March 2008. The full text is available on the *Guardian* website: www.guardian. co.uk

The 'common-law marriage' myth

Information from NatCen

People are confused about the legal consequences of living together outside marriage, according to the latest British Social Attitudes report, published today by NatCen. Despite a government-funded media campaign three years ago, half of adults still believe (wrongly) that there is such a thing as 'common-law marriage', which gives cohabitants the same rights as married couples.

Half of adults still believe (wrongly) that there is such a thing as 'common-law marriage', which gives cohabitants the same rights as married couples

Cohabitation remains a popular choice of relationship in Britain: more than one-third of people (36%) have cohabited in the past, and one in nine (11%) now do so. But cohabiting couples do not have the same legal rights as those who are married and in 2004, the government funded a campaign aimed at raising awareness of this, accompanied by considerable media coverage.

The report finds that:
⇨ Despite the campaign to raise awareness, half of people (51%) still believe (wrongly) that there is such a thing as 'common-law marriage' which gives cohabitants the same rights as married couples.
⇨ Only four in ten people (38%) correctly know that this is untrue. This is almost identical to the proportion of people who thought this in 2000, despite the campaigns that have taken place.

⇨ Cohabitants are no more or less knowledgeable than anyone else: 53% believe that common-law marriage exists, and 39% correctly say that it does not.

Few current cohabitants have taken steps to safeguard their position:
⇨ Around one in six (15%) of those who own their accommodation have a written agreement about their share in the ownership.
⇨ One in five (19%) have sought advice about their legal position.

There is strong public support for legal reform so that cohabiting couples in certain circumstances are treated in the same way as married couples. Public support for treating married and cohabiting couples equally increases as the relationship lengthens, particularly when children are involved:
⇨ Nine in ten people (89%) think that a cohabiting partner should have a right to financial provision on separation if the relationship has been a long-term one, includes children and has involved prioritising one partner's career over another.
⇨ Only four in ten people (38%) think that a cohabiting partner should have a right to financial

provision if the relationship only lasted two years and involves no children.

Professor Anne Barlow, co-author, comments:

'The myth that there is something called common-law marriage that gives cohabiting couples legal rights lives on, despite the media exposure of the last few years.

'There is little appetite for maintaining the deep legal divisions drawn between married and unmarried cohabiting families. The Law Commission should bear this in mind in their review of current legislation.'

Note
This summarises 'Cohabitation and the law: myths, money and the media' by Anne Barlow, Carole Burgoyne, Elizabeth Clery and Janet Smithson, in *British Social Attitudes: the 24th Report*, published by Sage for NatCen.
23 January 2008

⇨ The above information is reprinted with kind permission from NatCen, the National Centre for Social Research. Visit www.natcen.ac.uk for more information.
© NatCen

Why adultery can help save a marriage

Therapist is under fire for saying that cheating on your spouse can be more of a blessing than a sin

By Amelia Hill, Social Affairs Correspondent

A controversial self-help book for married philanderers claims most adulterers are good, kind people. It says affairs can help a marriage and that those who stray should never admit it because the truth can cause even more damage.

'Cheating on your spouse isn't a moral act, but most men and women who have affairs are good people who made a mistake,' said Mira Kirshenbaum, author of *When Good People Have Affairs*, published this week. 'They never thought it would happen to them but, suddenly, they're in this complicated, dangerous situation. We all agree that infidelity is a mistake. But once you've crossed the line, what then?'

Kirshenbaum has been criticised by her peers for saying cheats deserve sympathy and understanding. 'Adulterers are neither kind nor good people, so what sort of sympathy are we supposed to give them?' said Leila Collins, a psychologist who has given relationship counselling for 15 years. 'A good person doesn't betray their loved ones. A good person who is unsatisfied in their relationship ends it before starting a new one.'

Kirshenbaum, clinical director of the Chestnut Hill Institute, a centre for relationship therapy and research in Boston, Massachusetts, admits that infidelity is a controversial topic to address sympathetically. 'But these people are suffering terribly and need to be relieved of their sense of guilt and shame because those emotions are paralysing,' she said.

Those who have affairs are seeking real happiness and love in their lives, believes Kirshenbaum, who has been treating couples and individuals for 30 years and has written 10 books on relationships. 'Until now, the story of these men and women has never been told,' she said. 'Shame and fear have kept it in the closet and so they haven't had the understanding that might save them from ruining the lives of everyone involved.'

She believes that society's refusal to have a sympathetic discussion of infidelity has meant that the positive sides of betraying a spouse have been ignored. 'Sometimes an affair can be the best way for the person who has been unfaithful to get the information and impetus to change,' she said. 'I'm not encouraging affairs, but underlying the complicated mess is a kind of deep and delicate wisdom. It's an insight that something isn't working and needs to change.'

Her views reflect the plotline of Adrian Lyne's 2002 film, *Unfaithful*, in which Richard Gere's love for his wife, Diane Lane, is rekindled by her affair with a younger man, Olivier Martinez. 'If handled right, an affair can be therapeutic, give clarity and jolt people from their inertia,' she said. 'You could think of it as a radical but necessary medical procedure. If your marriage is in cardiac arrest, an affair can be a defibrillator.'

Kirshenbaum believes there are 17 reasons why people have affairs, including the see-if affair, the distraction affair and the sexual-panic affair. To help people decide whether their infidelity should spell the end of their marriage, she lists a few that she believes do indicate the relationship is over – and those that do not. 'You should stay with your partner if your affair is a heating-up-your-marriage affair, let's-kill-this-relationship-and-see-if-it-comes-back-to-life affair, do-I-still-have-it affair, accidental affair, revenge affair or midlife-crisis affair,' said Kirshenbaum.

'But you need to think carefully about whether to stay with your primary partner if your affair is of the following kinds: the break-out-into-selfhood affair, unmet-need affair, having-experiences-I-missed-out-on affair, surrogate-therapy affair, ejector-seat affair,' she said.

Kirshenbaum is adamant that an adulterer must never confess – not even if their partner asks directly. 'This is the one area in which the truth usually creates far more damage in the long run,' she said. 'A lot of people confess because they feel they just have to be honest. Well, honesty is great. But it's a very abstract moral

principle. A much more concrete, and much higher, moral principle is not hurting people. And when you confess to having an affair, you are hurting someone. If you care that much about honesty, figure out who you want to be with, commit to that relationship and devote the rest of your life to making it the most honest relationship you can,' she said.

There are two huge exceptions to not telling. 'If you're having an affair and you haven't practised safe sex,

you have to tell,' she said. 'You also have to tell if discovery is imminent or likely. If it's clear that you're going to be found out, it's better for you to make the confession first.'

Another reason for not telling is that it makes it far more difficult for a remorseful adulterer to return to the fold. 'If your partner will find out about your affair, your whole future happiness together depends on whether he's basically vengeful or basically merciful,' she said.

Kirshenbaum's opinion on what constitutes a happy ending is also controversial. Divorce, she believes, can be the path to a bright future. 'Sometimes – many times, in fact – divorce is worth it,' she said. 'It plays an important function. It gets us out of misery-making marriages and we have a chance of finding happiness somewhere else.'

⇨ This article first appeared in *The Observer*, 8 June 2008.

© *Guardian Newspapers Limited 2008*

Cohabitation

Information from Resolution

If you are living with someone without being married you might think you have similar rights to married couples if the relationship breaks down or one of you dies. You would be wrong. There is no such thing as a common-law marriage and cohabitants have very few rights that arise out of the relationship. You can't for example, claim maintenance from a cohabitant or former cohabitant for your own benefit.

If you live in a property in your partner's sole name
You have no automatic right to a share. You would have to establish a right by showing that:

⇨ You contributed to the purchase of the property, in which case the court would divide up the proceeds in the proportion in which you both contributed; or

⇨ You and your partner agreed that you would have a share and you

acted on that or you made direct financial contributions, in which case the court would divide up the proceeds in such a way as is fair taking account of your financial arrangements throughout your relationship; or

⇨ Your partner promised that you would have a share and you acted on that, in which case the court might transfer the property, give you the right to stay there or award you a fair share of the proceeds.

The strength of your case will depend on what evidence you have. But it can be very difficult, costly and time-consuming to establish such a right.

If you live in a property that is held in joint names with your partner
Your position depends on whether you own it as 'beneficial joint tenants' or 'tenants in common'.

⇨ Sometimes the solicitor who dealt with your purchase will not have specified either of these. In these circumstances it will be presumed that you have equal shares unless you are able to establish something different based on the sort of principles described above. You should check.

⇨ If you own the property as 'beneficial joint tenants' you own half each and nothing that either of you have done during your relationship affects this.

⇨ If you own the property as 'tenants in common' then the size of your share should have been specified. You should check. If they have not been specified you will have to establish the size of your share based on similar principles as described above. Where the documents are clear that will stand unless you can show that there has been fraud or mistake.

⇨ You are not entitled to maintenance from your partner.

If you and your partner have children together
⇨ The father will only automatically have parental responsibility if he registered as the father on the birth certificate after 1 December 2003. Otherwise he needs the formal written agreement of the mother or an order from the court.

⇨ If you are the main carer for the children, you can make financial claims on behalf of the children under Schedule 1 Children Act 1989. You and the children may be able to stay in the house whilst they are dependent, regardless of who owns the property, or the court can make orders for lump sums to provide for housing or for other specific capital needs of the children. In deciding this the court would look at whether this would be in the best interests of the children. Generally you will have to repay capital once the children are 18 or have finished their education. You can also get child support through the Child Support Agency and in some cases through the court.

If your partner dies and has not made a will

⇨ You are not entitled to any part of their estate unless you own the property as 'beneficial joint tenants' in which case it would pass to you.

⇨ Otherwise your partner's estate will go to their next of kin. This could be a spouse if they have never divorced. If your partner has children, their spouse would get the first £125,000, personal possessions and income from half the rest. The remaining half would go to their children who would then get the other half when the spouse dies. If your partner is divorced or never been married, all property would then go to their children. You could be out on the street.

⇨ If you own a property with your partner as 'beneficial tenants in common' your partner's share will go to his next of kin as above. You might have to sell to buy them out.

⇨ If you are left with nothing you would have to make a claim against your partner's estate on the basis that you lived together for two years prior to the date of death or that you were wholly or partly dependent on them. This can be difficult, costly and time-consuming.

This is why its really important to make a will.

Cohabitation contracts

You can enter into a cohabitation contract which is an enforceable agreement setting out what you would both want to happen in the event of your separation. These agreements are likely to be enforceable.

See www.advicenow.org.uk/ livingtogether

⇨ The above information is re-printed with kind permission from Resolution. Visit www.resolution.org. uk for more information.

© Resolution

The changing family

Family structure has changed dramatically over past decade, finds new research

The number of cohabiting couple families in the UK increased by 65 per cent between 1996 and 2006 and the number of married couple families fell by 4 per cent, according to a report published this week by a team of researchers from the Office of National Statistics (ONS), LSE and Warwick University.

The report, *Focus on Families 2007*, was carried out for the ONS by Professor Mike Murphy, professor of demography at LSE, who looked at the relationship between family living arrangement and health; Linda Pickard, research fellow at LSE, who looked at unpaid care and the family; Hannah McConnell, Ben Wilson and Steve Smallwood, ONS; and Richard Lampard, Warwick University.

The researchers found that the total number of families in the UK reached 17.1 million in 2006, compared with 16.5 million in 1996. However, the number of families headed by a married couple fell by half a million between 1996 and 2006, to just over 12 million. At the same time both lone-mother and cohabiting couple families increased so that they now total 2.3 million each.

Key findings include:

⇨ In 2001 half of cohabiting couple families were headed by a person under 35.

⇨ Lone-mother families tend to be younger than lone-father families by approximately ten years.

⇨ One in three lone mothers in the UK were aged under 35, whereas less than one in ten lone fathers were under 35.

⇨ Younger generations are more likely to cohabit.

⇨ Stepfamilies containing dependent children are even more likely to be cohabiting couple families.

⇨ 17-year-olds are most likely to be in education if in married couple non-stepfamilies.

⇨ Those with no qualifications marry early but appear least likely to marry.

⇨ Partnership continues to be the healthiest state – there are health benefits associated with partnership, especially marriage, but there are variations by sex. In particular, older single women have better health than married women on many indicators of health status.

⇨ The majority of unpaid care is family care, especially when provided for long hours. Around 1.2 million working-age adults in Britain provide intense unpaid care for a spouse, parent or others for 20 hours a week or more, either inside or outside the household.

⇨ Adults who are married are approximately twice as likely to provide intense care for an ill, disabled or elderly relative or friend as those who are cohabiting.

⇨ London has the highest proportion of lone parents.

⇨ London and Northern Ireland had the lowest proportions of stepfamilies and Yorkshire and the Humber had the highest proportion of stepfamilies.

⇨ The largest families are in Northern Ireland.

5 October 2007

⇨ The above information is re-printed with kind permission from the London School of Economics and Political Science. Visit www.lse. ac.uk for more information.

© London School of Economics and Political Science

Love by numbers

'My parents have said I do not have to have an arranged marriage if I don't want to but it will hurt them deeply if I don't. What should I do?'

My parents have said I do not have to have an arranged marriage if I don't want to but it will hurt them deeply if I don't. What should I do?

Many people still have arranged marriages, especially in Asia, Africa and the Middle East. Now that

A study of 586 married women in Sichuan in China found that women in love matches were happier than those in arranged marriages. Both types of marriage had higher ratings the longer the union lasted

divorce rates are so high in western countries, a bit of arranging seems more attractive and is essentially what dating agencies and websites try to do. Arranged marriages have had a bad press, though, being associated with forced marriages and childhood betrothals. Historically they were for the advancement of families rather than the happiness of individuals. Men were typically older than their wives (sometimes ancient) and

By Dr Luisa Dillner

couples were matched for religious belief, caste, money, height (taller men only, please) and social standing.

Arguments for arranged marriages hinge on the frivolity of young people choosing looks and sexual chemistry over prospects. The unrealistic feelings in these 'love matches' are bashed by the reality of domesticity which causes many to bale out or become progressively unhappy. Arranged marriages are said to 'start cold' and heat up. There are no expectations of happiness, but a duty felt to those who have brought them together, so working at the relationship is a given. At the risk of being trivial, you could marry someone you will never find sexually attractive. But Amit Batabyal, Professor of Economics at the Rochester Institute of Technology, who has researched the economics of arranged marriages, says modern ones are more flexible. Parents and matchmakers are more like consultants than marriage enforcers.

You'd hope that arranged marriage would reduce your risk of divorce and make you happier. Batabyal says divorce rates are higher in countries with mostly 'love matches', which may be because divorce is limited in countries where arranged marriages prevail. Reports in the *Times of India*

say divorce rates in Mumbai are 40% and also rising in Goa, though the website divorcerates.org says that India's divorce rate is still around 1%.

Arguments for arranged marriages hinge on the frivolity of young people choosing looks and sexual chemistry over prospects

So, are arranged marriages any happier? A study of 586 married women in Sichuan in China found that women in love matches were happier than those in arranged marriages. Both types of marriage had higher ratings the longer the union lasted.

If you choose a love match, it will be hard for your parents. You could ask them to suggest people without being obligated to marry them. Agree what you will do if you meet someone yourself and what you are looking for. Try to avoid falling for an Elvis impersonator, as this would be too much for most parents to deal with.

9 August 2008

© Guardian Newspapers Limited 2008

What is a forced marriage?

Information from the Forced Marriage Unit

What is forced marriage?

A marriage must be entered into with the full and free consent of both people. Everyone involved should feel that they have a choice.

An arranged marriage is not the same as a forced marriage. In an arranged marriage, the families take a leading role in choosing the marriage partner. The marriage is entered into freely by both people.

An arranged marriage is not the same as a forced marriage. In an arranged marriage, the families take a leading role in choosing the marriage partner. The marriage is entered into freely by both people

---

However, in some cases, one or both people are 'forced' into a marriage that their families want. A forced marriage is a marriage conducted without the valid consent of both people, where pressure or abuse is used.

You might be put under both physical pressure (when someone threatens to or actually does hurt you), or emotional pressure (for example, when someone makes you feel like you're bringing shame on your family) to get married.

In some cases people may be taken abroad without knowing that they are to be married. When they arrive in the country their passports may be taken by their family to try and stop them from returning home.

Forced marriage is an abuse of human rights, and a form of domestic violence and child abuse.

If you or someone you know is being forced into a marriage, help and advice is available.

What to do . . .

If you or someone you know is being forced into marriage either in the UK or abroad, you can contact the Forced Marriage Unit (FMU).

The Forced Marriage Unit is there to help people who are being forced into marriage. The FMU's caseworkers understand the issues, the family pressures and how difficult it is to talk about these situations.

The Forced Marriage Unit offers confidential support and information.

You have a right to choose... and the Forced Marriage Unit is there to help you.

You can:

⇨ Call: (+44) (0)20 7008 0151 between 9am and 5pm, Monday to Friday

⇨ Emergency Duty Officer (out of office hours): (+44) (0)20 7008 1500

⇨ Or e-mail: fmu@fco.gov.uk

Find out more about the work of the Forced Marriage Unit at: www.fco.gov.uk/forcedmarriage

You are not alone . . .

When you are caught in this situation it is not unusual to feel completely alone... but you are not. Each year, more than 250 cases of forced marriage are reported to us.

Around 85% of those cases involve women who have been forced into marriage and some 15% of cases involve men. And there are many more cases – involving both men and women – that don't get reported.

Narina's story (now 21)

'I felt that I had no option. Once they had taken me out of the country there was nothing I could do. I had no contact with anyone but the family. My mother was caught between my feelings and the community's expectations. They made me feel that I would dishonour my family if I didn't marry him.'

Narina was 18 when her parents took her back home for a family holiday. She was kept in the family home and wasn't allowed out on her own. Finally, she and her sister managed to run away and contacted the British Consulate, who found her a place to stay and helped her contact her friends in the UK. She eventually came home and with the help of a women's refuge and her friends, has built a new life for herself and her sister.

Raj's story (now 29)

'People don't realise that men can also find themselves in this situation. I don't know if I could have told anyone even if I'd had the chance to. It's not exactly macho, is it, admitting that you were held hostage by your family and forced to marry someone you'd never even met...'

Raj was forced into a marriage. When he'd finally returned to the UK, it took him 3 years to get out of it. He may have been able to avoid the financial and emotional turmoil of divorce if he had known about the support and help at hand.

Sola's story (now 24)

'My parents took me back home, saying they wanted me to learn more about our culture and to experience life there. I had no idea they had marriage planned for me. If I had known I would have run away or found help earlier.'

Sola thought she was going overseas to find out more about her culture. However, when she arrived, her family told her that she had to get married. After the marriage she managed to come back to the UK with help from the British Consulate. She has been going to counselling to help her cope with depression and anxiety.

A forced marriage is a marriage conducted without the valid consent of both people, where pressure or abuse is used

---

Lena's story (now 19)

'My father found out that I had a boyfriend and that changed everything in our family. He literally kept me prisoner in the house, wouldn't let me see my friends and then started planning my wedding – to a man I had never met! He said that I had to follow our customs, and there would be no discussion. I didn't have any other way out...'

When Lena's father found out about her boyfriend, he was so angry that he cut off her hair. He told her that having a boyfriend was against their culture. She would have to marry the man he chose and have a virginity test. Lena was so scared that she took an overdose. Fortunately she recovered in hospital.

Frequently asked questions

What happens when you call the FMU helpline?

You will talk to an experienced caseworker who will listen and offer you confidential support and information. You can discuss your options with them. We can give you information on your rights and the services available to support you. We will not contact your family.

I can't afford to leave home. So, how is being homeless with no money a better life than a forced marriage?

If you are a woman, you can go to a refuge. A refuge is a safe environment which can provide you with emotional and practical help such as access to counselling, and sorting out benefits and housing.

You will be encouraged to become independent and to make your own decisions about your future. If you are male, call us to discuss your options.

How can you guarantee my safety?

While we cannot guarantee safety, we can put you in contact with agencies whose job it is to help protect you. You should always call the police if you are in immediate danger. Refuges can provide you with somewhere safe to stay if you choose to leave home.

If I think I might be forced into a marriage when I go abroad, what should I do?

Think very carefully before you decide to go abroad. Once you are abroad, it will be much harder to get help. If you decide to go, please contact us at the FMU. Make sure you take the address and contact numbers of a trusted friend and of the High Commission/Embassy in the country you are visiting (call the FMU for this number or go to www.fco.gov.uk) and keep them somewhere safe. Take some money with you in pounds and in the local currency, a spare mobile phone and a copy of your passport and tickets.

What happens if I am abroad and realise that I am being forced into a marriage?

You or a trusted friend should contact the nearest British Consulate, Embassy or High Commission. They will contact the FMU in the UK and arrange for assistance.

What happens if I'm abroad and manage to run away, but I don't have enough money to fly home?

If you haven't got the money, and you can't borrow it from a friend or relative, the Foreign & Commonwealth Office may in some circumstances be able to loan you the money for a ticket. But you'll have to pay this back when you get home.

How long will it take before I can come back to the UK and where will I stay while arrangements are being made?

We will try and make arrangements for you to come back as soon as possible. However, if you do have to stay abroad for any length of time, we will try to find you a suitable place to stay.

If I'm abroad, what will happen if I don't have my passport?

Provided you are a British national, we can issue you with an emergency passport.

I got married overseas. Is my marriage valid in the UK?

If your marriage is seen as valid in the country where it took place, in many cases it will be valid in the UK. You must talk to a solicitor, whether you had a religious or civil marriage. Religious divorce is not valid in the UK.

Can you still help me if I'm under 16?

Yes we can. Please call the FMU to discuss these options.

⇨ The above information is reprinted with kind permission from the Forced Marriage Unit. Visit www.fco.gov.uk/forcedmarriage for more.

Escaping forced marriage

Information from the Foreign and Commonwealth Office

Imagine you're an average teenage girl. Maybe you're worried about getting good A level results or even GCSE grades.

Then one day you're forced to travel to your family's homeland. When you get there your family takes your passport and phone. You're locked in the home and beaten before being forced to marry a man you've never even met. And then you're raped on your wedding night.

What makes all this worse is your family isn't trying to help you – they are the ones who've led you here.

Forced Marriage Unit

Our Forced Marriage Unit (FMU) deals with cases like this every week. It's run in partnership with the Home Office and is the only government unit in the world dedicated to investigating and helping people escape forced marriages.

People like 'Farah' – she was held against her will and almost forced into marriage in Pakistan.

Tricked

Despite her family agreeing that she could marry her boyfriend in the UK, they tricked her into travelling to Pakistan telling her that her grandfather was dying. When she arrived her family confiscated her mobile phone and told her she was going to be married to a stranger in the next few days.

She was regularly beaten by her own brother for refusing to accept this forced marriage.

Suspicion

But her boyfriend back in the UK suspected something was wrong. He contacted us and his local police to report that Farah was being held against her will.

The FMU and staff in the High Commission in Islamabad contacted Farah on the family phone. When we spoke to her she said she wasn't being badly treated or forced into marriage, but we suspected that she was unable to talk freely. So we left our contact details with her and didn't close the case.

Pleaded

Later that same day, Farah contacted us from a friend's house. She told us the truth and said that during the previous call her brother was in the room writing down the things she should say. She pleaded with us to rescue her from the nightmare in which she had found herself.

Our rescue operation swung into action and within 48 hours our staff had got her out and brought her back to Islamabad. She had visible physical injuries where her brother and mother had attacked her and was extremely distressed.

Back in the UK the FMU arranged for her boyfriend to send her the money for a flight home. The next day they were reunited at the airport and they are now happily married.

Did you know?

⇨ The FMU deals with around 300 cases a year.

⇨ One-third of the victims are under 18.

⇨ Fifteen per cent of the victims are men.

⇨ We have six full-time staff in London who work with our consular staff around the world.

⇨ Whilst most of our cases are in Pakistan and Bangladesh we also deal with cases in unexpected locations like Ireland and Norway.

⇨ We can also help people in the UK – you don't need to be overseas to contact us.

⇨ If you are a victim of forced marriage we can try and stop your spouse getting a visa to come to the UK.

If you know of any case of forced marriage, or if you want confidential advice, contact FMU on 020-7008 0151 or email fmu@fco.gov.uk

⇨ The above information is reprinted with kind permission from the Foreign and Commonwealth Office. Visit www.fco.gov.uk for more information.

© Crown copyright

'Thousands' of British girls in forced marriages

There is growing concern thousands of British girls are being taken out of schools and forced into marriages after new figures hinted the problem was far worse than previously thought

There is growing concern thousands of British girls are being taken out of schools and forced into marriages after new figures hinted the problem was far worse than previously thought.

'This is not a culturally sensitive issue, this is an abhorrent act which we must stand together on'

A study by the Home Office found there were more than 300 inquiries in the town of Luton in one year and the issue is likely to be widespread across the country.

The Government's forced marriage unit deals with that number of cases per year, but the known scale of the problem may just be the tip of the iceberg, management consultant Dr Nazia Khanum said.

Dr Khanum, whose report is to be published, said: 'Three hundred

By Sophie Borland

inquiries are made to the voluntary sector per year in Luton alone.

'The forced marriage unit deal with 300 hardcore cases a year. If you follow the examples of rape and domestic violence, where only 10 per cent to 12 per cent of cases are reported, it's a reasonable assumption it is the tip of the iceberg.'

Meanwhile Baroness Warsi, shadow minister for community cohesion and social action, has called for such marriages to be treated as crimes to send a clear signal they were intolerable.

Speaking on a GMTV programme, she said society had realised domestic violence was not a taboo subject and the Government needed to give girls protection against the forced marriages.

She said: 'As a society we draw a line in the sand.

'This is not a culturally sensitive issue, this is an abhorrent act which we must stand together on.'

Earlier this month it was disclosed some 33 girls were missing from Bradford's schools after extensive efforts to locate them. It is feared the children have been pressured into forced marriages and the Government also has concerns about 14 further areas which are suspected of having high rates of so-called 'honour violence'.

The known scale of the problem may just be the tip of the iceberg

Kevin Brennan, Children's Minister, told the Commons Home Affairs Select Committee, which has been investigating forced marriages, Bradford City Council lost track of 205 youngsters last year. Further inquiries had established the whereabouts of 172 – leaving 33 unaccounted for.

16 March 2008

© *Telegraph Group Ltd, London 2008*

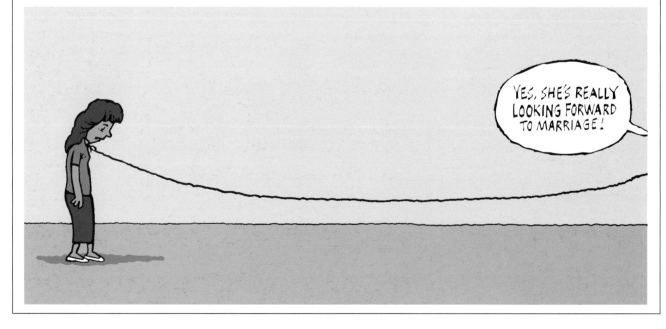

Divorce and dissolution of civil partnership

Information from Resolution

The legal process of ending a marriage or civil partnership can have a major emotional and financial impact on all family members.

Resolution members aim to help separating couples achieve a constructive settlement of their differences in a way which avoids protracted arguments and promotes co-operation between parents in decisions concerning children.

> **To get a divorce in England and Wales, you need to show that you have been married for more than a year and that the marriage has broken down**

If you are having problems in your marriage or partnership, you should first consider whether these difficulties could be resolved with the help of a trained relationship counsellor. Organisations such as Relate could help you: www.relate.org.uk

If you do decide to divorce or dissolve your partnership, a lawyer will be able to advise and guide you through the process. A lawyer will outline your options at every stage and give you the information to make your own decisions.

NB: The process for dissolution of civil partnership is the same as for divorce. Where the term 'divorce' is used in this article it should be taken to include dissolution of civil partnership. The only exception is adultery which is a specific legal term relating to heterosexual sex and which cannot therefore be used as grounds for dissolving a civil partnership. If your partner is unfaithful the grounds for dissolution would instead be unreasonable behaviour.

Reasons for an application for divorce

To get a divorce in England and Wales, you need to show that you have been married for more than a year and that the marriage has broken down.

The marriage must have broken down for one of these reasons:

⇨ Your spouse has committed adultery and you find it intolerable to live together.

⇨ Your spouse has behaved in such a way that you cannot reasonably be expected to live together.

⇨ You have been separated for two years and your spouse agrees to divorce.

⇨ You have been separated for five years.

⇨ Your spouse deserted you more than two years ago.

The reason for the breakdown of the marriage forms the basis of the divorce application, known as the 'petition'. If more than one of the above reasons applies, your solicitor will advise on which is most suitable to your circumstances and what additional information the court needs.

If you or your spouse has committed adultery, it is not usually necessary to name the other person. If the petition is based on the behaviour of your spouse, you will need to give some limited examples of their behaviour and how it has affected you.

These details (known as 'particulars') can be agreed with your spouse in advance, to avoid increasing any conflict between you both.

If you carry on living together for more than six months after either the

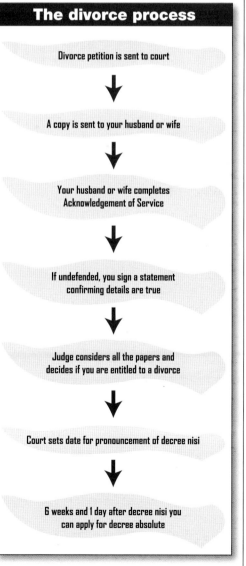

The divorce process

Divorce petition is sent to court

↓

A copy is sent to your husband or wife

↓

Your husband or wife completes Acknowledgement of Service

↓

If undefended, you sign a statement confirming details are true

↓

Judge considers all the papers and decides if you are entitled to a divorce

↓

Court sets date for pronouncement of decree nisi

↓

6 weeks and 1 day after decree nisi you can apply for decree absolute

last act of unreasonable behaviour or the discovery of the last act of adultery, then you cannot get a divorce based on this. Similarly, a period of separation is discounted if you live together again for a period of six months.

What the divorce process involves

The divorce is begun by sending to the court the petition, your marriage certificate and the court fee (or a claim for exemption from the fee if you are receiving legal aid).

If you have children, you will also need to give details of their names and dates of birth, where they are living, which schools they attend and what arrangements have been made for their care. See our fact sheet on *Contact with children after divorce, dissolution of civil partnership, or separation.*

A copy of the petition and statement of arrangements for children is sent to your spouse who is required to complete an Acknowledgment of Service saying whether or not he/she agrees with the divorce. Provided he/she does not contest it, following this:

⇨ You then confirm that all the details are true and the court grants a Decree Nisi if satisfied that the ground for divorce is established.

⇨ After six weeks and one day, it can be converted into a Decree Absolute, which marks the end of the marriage.

⇨ If the spouse who issues the divorce (called the petitioner) does not apply for the Decree Absolute after the six-week period, the other spouse (the respondent) can apply for a court hearing to get it. However, in some circumstances the divorce can be held up until arrangements for any children and financial matters are agreed.

⇨ The petitioner can stop the process at any time before the Decree Nisi and if both parties agree it can be stopped after Decree Nisi provided that it is before Decree Absolute.

If the divorce is defended, the position is much more complex.

You will also need to settle financial matters relating to the family home, maintenance, pensions, and any savings and investments. The legal term for this is 'Ancillary Relief' – see our fact sheet on *Financial arrangements on divorce and dissolution of civil partnership.*

The time it takes to get a divorce will vary according to the complexity of each case and the practice of the particular court. Even the most straightforward divorces will take between four and six months.

⇨ The above information is re-printed with kind permission from Resolution. Visit www.resolution.org. uk for more information.

© Resolution

The end of a marriage

No one ever expects to be divorced or separated, and when it happens nothing can prepare you for the pain and devastation it causes

Divorce is one of the most painful experiences you can go through because it impacts every aspect of your life. In addition to the rejection and sense of loss, there is the burden of shame and failure. Your past and your future seem to be wiped out in one blow, and functioning in the present demands every ounce of your energy and focus. So how do you cope?

Shattered dreams

My marriage was filled with tension from the beginning. My husband was in the defence force which took him away for two or three weeks at a time and then he would come back to suburban life. It was quite difficult for him to adapt, I think. I was working and very involved in the church. We hadn't managed to conceive which I found hard to cope with as the biological clock was ticking and he would not consider adoption. Eventually we effectively led two separate lives.

Then we moved to another area where he started a new job and we had a much happier time for a couple of years. I felt that things were coming right and was hoping that we were going to be able to start a family. But one night my husband came home and said he was moving out. Initially I was stunned, and then I started questioning him and asking what was wrong, what had happened.

I found out that he had become close to a married woman we were friends with at church. She and my husband both enjoyed keeping fit and had been running together. I found out too that while I was at work they had been meeting in my house. My initial shock turned into anger then.

Over so soon

The divorce proceedings were very quick. I felt very awkward telling a solicitor, a stranger, all about my private life and I didn't always feel that he was on my side. But it was all over within four months of my husband moving out. Three weeks after that he had married this woman, who had also divorced her husband, so it had all been planned by them.

A friend of mine said that at least I had everything happen all at once – I'd gone through the divorce and the remarriage of my partner and now I could move on. But it wasn't that simple.

Learning to cope

I don't know how you really cope with something like this especially as I viewed marriage as a lifetime commitment. You have to learn to cope just by getting through each day at a time. I kept working because I knew I had to support myself. And my friends were very good helping me with practical things and just letting me talk and talk, to rattle on as you do. But there was a long period of time when I was just completely and utterly stunned and couldn't feel anything. However, my faith and the support of my friends kept me going. I tried to make sense of why everything had happened. What had I done? What hadn't I done?

I lost all my self-confidence and self-esteem and became depressed trying to cope with my loneliness. Consequently I ended up having some counselling. I really wrestled with being a single woman again and of being denied the opportunity to have children, as I so badly wanted to have a family of my own.

Liz

Starting again

We had been married 13 years when I found that I just couldn't take any more of my wife's behaviour. I had been running my own business, trying to build a house, facing financial difficulties and undergoing cancer treatment, yet my wife only seemed to be concerned with going on jaunts overseas to see art exhibitions.

She was an artist and when she did well from commissions, she kept the money to herself instead of helping to pay our mortgage. Then we decided to sell our house and get something smaller. We made a good profit but instead of using it as a buffer for the future, my wife decided to once again travel alone.

This time while she was away I tried to call her to discuss a minor matter. The friends she was staying with said that she was unavailable and wouldn't give me a contact number for her. When she returned I said that I was moving out. She didn't seem too distressed. I found out later that a few weeks after I left, a man came from overseas and moved in with her.

What next?

I had been living with such uncertainty, dishonesty and distrust for such a long time that the anger had been welling inside me. I told my wife that she could keep the house if we would agree not to have anything more to do with each other. I felt at this point that getting away was a positive move, and I had a tremendous sense of relief. But I had nothing except my suitcase.

Many of our friends cut me off. I didn't want to badmouth my wife and they assumed that I had just abandoned her. My mother had been through a divorce herself but she didn't give me much emotional support and I had just a couple of friends who had been through divorce who helped me get back on my feet.

I spent a lot of time just working very, very hard. Eventually I found a new church where they had a men's group. Some of these guys had been through divorces and for the first time I could be completely open. I was able to start to trust people again as I talked through what had happened. But I think men generally find it very difficult to discuss these things; particularly British men who are told to have a stiff upper lip and guard their feelings. If they chat at all it is at the pub where things will be joked about and that undermines the deep emotions that are really being felt.

David

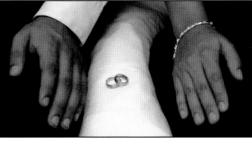
Divorce and separation can be devastating

Dealing with emotions
Anger
⇨ Acknowledge and accept your anger.
⇨ Identify the reason – am I feeling hurt, frustrated or threatened?
⇨ Take steps to deal with the cause or get help to talk about it.
⇨ Decide on a strategy to stay in control for when your anger is triggered.
⇨ Do not seek ways of taking revenge: it will not bring healing for you and will cause more damage.
⇨ Don't suppress your anger. Internalised anger is not resolved anger. It must be faced and managed; otherwise it will manifest in health problems like headaches and will cause depression.
⇨ Find a safe outlet for your anger

such as kneading bread, beating a punchbag or pillow, or throwing glass bottles into the bottle bank and hearing them smash.
⇨ Talk to a trusted friend or a counsellor.
⇨ Try writing down your feelings. Using words to express how you feel is better than allowing your anger to be acted out. You might like to write a letter to someone you are angry with – but don't send it. Instead burn it, and allow your feelings to go up in smoke.
⇨ Channel any anger towards your own healing, growth and learning; become determined to be a happier and stronger person.
⇨ Find projects you can take up which will help you vent your anger healthily – joining a health club, DIY jobs, taking up a new hobby.
⇨ When you are ready, forgive the people who hurt you.

Loneliness
⇨ Get involved in someone else's life – invite friends round, share meals.
  ⇨ Look at the way you live – does it encourage loneliness? If so, change. Don't blame others for your loneliness.
  ⇨ Visit others who are in need: elderly, sick or disabled.
  ⇨ Join a group of volunteers.
  ⇨ Take up a hobby or join a class.
⇨ Don't stifle the issue with drugs, alcohol, overeating or oversleeping.
⇨ Increase your contacts, by writing, phoning or talking to new people.
⇨ Appreciate yourself.
⇨ Have an encouraging book or music near your bed for lonely times at night.
⇨ Plan your time alone. Avoid feeling down on a Friday night or Bank Holiday by planning in a treat for yourself – rent a film and watch it with your favourite snacks, visit friends or make a trip to a gallery or museum.
⇨ Celebrate your achievements each day, no matter how trivial.
⇨ Live one day at a time.

Making decisions
I'll always remember the day he told me. It was Easter Sunday and I was

six months pregnant. He said that he was seeing someone from work. He didn't want me to tell anyone because he knew everyone would give him a hard time. He left and didn't come back till the Tuesday.

I don't know what I did in those intervening days. I was very, very shocked and felt humiliated with the deceit and not having seen it coming. But I immediately started thinking practically. There was no going back after what he had said. The shutters went down. He had made his decision so I had to look to the future and my baby.

Is this for real?

We had been together for about 14 years, since I was 17. I did ask myself how this was happening to me, but only briefly and in the sense of going over the past few months and making links in my head. I tortured myself with that a bit. I hadn't been suspicious of him at all. I had even overheard a telephone conversation and joked about it with him because it didn't occur to me to think along those lines.

I agreed to his suggestion that we wouldn't tell anyone until the baby was born. I think I agreed to most things at the time. I didn't want people fussing over me but he had things easy. He would stay with the girlfriend in the week and come back at the weekend and I was left to cover for him when people rang for him and wondered where he was. If I had my time again I don't think I would do his washing for him, as I did, and certainly not the ironing!

I think being pregnant actually made it easier in some ways. I had the baby to focus on and the most important thing was that the baby was all right. It was scary making decisions by myself. Being with one person for so long, I had got to the stage where I couldn't choose a dessert without asking his opinion. But once I found I could do it, I got a lot stronger.

So, in the long run, the divorce gave me back myself. I found I didn't have to rely on anyone for anything.

Once my baby was born, there was no time to celebrate. Within a week we had told everyone that my husband was leaving. And I had to go straight back to work because I had

How to help those going through divorce

⇨ Be prepared to accept them where they are, whether angry, upset or even relieved. Show them love and support. – Don't judge them.

⇨ Don't give your opinion on the other partner – the couple may still be reconciled and then your condemnation of the individual will affect your friendship.

⇨ Be inclusive in conversation – talking about your own partner may exclude them. Listen and follow their leading. They may or may not want to talk about the situation. Don't pry.

⇨ Don't make glib statements about how they can get over the situation. Clichés like 'Plenty more fish in the sea', or 'time is a great healer' are not appropriate in a time of grief and loss.

⇨ Offer practical help. Don't wait to be asked but suggest ways in which you can help with childcare, preparing meals, finding a reliable plumber, mechanic, cleaner or someone to do the ironing.

⇨ Bank holidays are particularly difficult, as are anniversaries, so try to find activities to involve the individual at those times.

⇨ They will need help long after the first few months. Be prepared to stay for the long haul.

to support myself. I think that is my one regret – that I didn't take more time to be with my baby.

I accepted my ex-husband's decision to end our marriage almost immediately. I think it took me a lot, lot longer to trust again, and not feel bad about myself.

Abigail

It couldn't be that bad

I didn't think it was over. He told me he was leaving and that he didn't love me any more, but I thought he'd got it all wrong and he would realise eventually and come back. There was disbelief that there could be anything that wrong that couldn't be put right. We had been married for 28 years. I thought he must be having a breakdown. It was a gentle departure. I helped him pack and sent him off with flowers and food. I gave him a hug. I thought he would live on his own, miss me and come back.

But time passed...

After six months a friend told me that my husband had been seeing another woman. I was devastated. That's when I knew it was the end. I was stunned and shocked, humiliated and very angry. I went past his house and saw the car. I wanted to crash into it but I realised just in time that I would

be the one in trouble, and it wasn't worth it. I didn't stop shaking for four months. The shock of it all was terrible, as was the sense of loneliness and fear of the future. I couldn't stop talking. I had lots of good friends and I would just go over and over the same thing to whoever would listen. It made me feel better if someone else knew. I wasn't expecting them to resolve it. Some things I knew I shouldn't say to people locally so I called my sister. Looking back I realised that I chose to say certain things to certain people – that no one person was burdened with everything.

Hindsight is a wonderful thing

I know now that there were things I could have handled differently in our marriage, mostly communication. But I don't think that there should have been a separation because of it. I can forgive him for not realising he had a problem with us and not dealing with it in a better way. But I find it hard coping with the fact that he broke up our family.

Jenny

⇨ The above information is re-printed with kind permission from Care for the Family. Visit www.careforthefamily.org.uk for more information.

© Care for the Family

Divorces

England and Wales rate at 26-year low

In 2007 the provisional divorce rate in England and Wales fell to 11.9 divorcing people per 1,000 married population compared with the 2006 figure of 12.2. The divorce rate is at its lowest level since 1981.

For the sixth consecutive year both men and women in their late twenties had the highest divorce rates of all five-year age groups. In 2007 there were 26.6 divorces per 1,000 married men aged 25-29 and 26.9 divorces per 1,000 married women aged 25-29.

Since 1997 the average age at divorce in England and Wales has risen from 40.2 to 43.7 years for men and from 37.7 to 41.2 years for women, partly reflecting the rise in age at marriage.

One in five men and women divorcing in 2007 had a previous marriage ending in divorce. This proportion has doubled in 27 years: in 1980 one in ten men and women divorcing had a previous marriage ending in divorce. Sixty-nine per cent of divorces were to couples where the marriage was the first for both parties.

For 68 per cent of divorces in 2007, the wife was granted the divorce. For all divorces granted to an individual (rather than jointly to both), behaviour was the most common fact proven.

United Kingdom

Between 2006 and 2007, the provisional number of divorces granted in the UK fell by 2.6 per cent to 144,220, from 148,141. This is the third consecutive fall in the number of UK divorces and the lowest number since 1977 (138,445). The figure is 20 per cent lower than the highest number of divorces, which peaked in 1993 (180,018).

The provisional number of divorces in England and Wales fell by 3.0 per cent to 128,534 in 2007. The number of divorces in Scotland decreased by 1.9 per cent from 13,014 in 2006 to 12,773 in 2007. Conversely, the

Office for National Statistics

provisional number of divorces in Northern Ireland increased to 2,913 in 2007, a 14 per cent increase from 2006 (2,565).

Source

Office for National Statistics; General Register Office for Scotland; Northern Ireland Statistics and Research Agency.

Notes

⇨ The term divorce here includes both dissolutions and annulments.
⇨ The average (mean) ages presented have not been standardised for age and therefore do not take account of the changing age structure of the population.

⇨ Rates for England and Wales in 2007 are provisional as they were produced using the 2006 mid-year marital status estimates. Marital status estimates for the UK are not available.
⇨ The Divorce Reform Act 1969 came into effect in England and Wales on 1 January 1971. The Act, subsequently consolidated in the Matrimonial Causes Act 1973, made it possible for the first time for divorce to be petitioned for on the couple's separation.
⇨ The Family Law (Scotland) Act 2006 came into effect on 4 May 2006. The Act reduced the separation periods for divorce with consent to one year (previously two years) and without consent to two years (previously five years). It also removed 'desertion' as a ground.
29 August 2008

⇨ The above information is re-printed with kind permission from the Office for National Statistics. Visit www.statistics.gov.uk for more information.

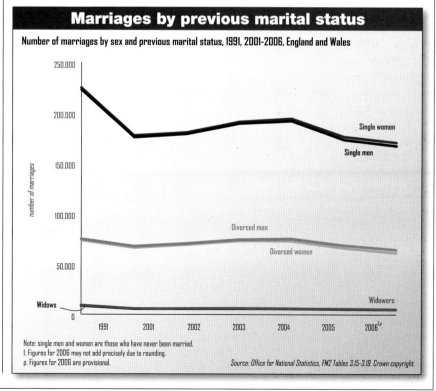

Marriages by previous marital status

Number of marriages by sex and previous marital status, 1991, 2001-2006, England and Wales

Single women

Single men

Divorced men

Divorced women

Widows

Widowers

Note: single men and women are those who have never been married.
1. Figures for 2006 may not add precisely due to rounding.
p. Figures for 2006 are provisional.

Source: Office for National Statistics, FM2 Tables 3.15-3.19. Crown copyright.

Legal jargon explained

Information from Divorce.co.uk

Here are some of the common terms related to divorce law that you may encounter.

Acknowledgement of service form
The form by which the respondent (or co-respondent) acknowledges having received the divorce petition.

Affidavit
A formal statement sworn on oath to be true by the person making it, usually in support of an application to the court, for example in relation to financial matters.

Ancillary relief
A general term for the possible financial orders that a court can make.

Answer
The formal defence to a divorce petition.

CAFCASS
The Children and Family Court Advisory and Support Service (formerly, the Court Welfare Service). A CAFCASS officer is a social worker who assists the court with matters relating to children and may prepare a report in certain types of proceedings. In disputed children proceedings, he or she will usually meet with both parents and the children in order to prepare a report for the court on what is in the child's best interests.

Clean break
A financial arrangement where it is agreed or ordered that the husband and wife will make no further claims against each other for capital or maintenance.

Conciliation
The historical term for mediation. See below.

Consent order
An order made by a court giving effect to the terms agreed between husband and wife.

Contact (formerly access)
The arrangement by which a child sees the parent, or other individual, with whom he or she does not live.

Co-respondent
A person with whom the respondent is alleged to have committed adultery. The law no longer requires that person to be named as a co-respondent in the divorce proceedings and a responsible solicitor will try to discourage you from doing so, as it is likely to create greater animosity and delay, and make the process more expensive in the long run.

Decree absolute
The final order of the court, which brings the marriage to an end.

Decree nisi
The provisional order indicating that the court is satisfied that the ground for divorce has been established.

District judge
A county court judge who deals with most of the divorce proceedings and usually with financial matters.

Domicile
The legal relationship between an individual and a country, usually arising from residence there with the intention of making it his or her permanent home.

Duxbury calculation
A formula for working out the lump sum appropriate for a clean break, based on the amount of maintenance payable and the life expectancy of the recipient, etc.

Family Proceedings Court
The name given to the division of the Magistrates' Court that deals with family law matters.

Financial dispute resolution appointment (FDR)
The second court appointment in ancillary relief proceedings when a judge looks at the offers made on a 'without prejudice' basis. Can, in more simple cases, sometimes be combined with the first appointment (below) to save costs and speed progress.

First appointment (or first directions appointment FDA)
The first court appointment in financial cases, when a judge considers what information is needed from each party in order to progress the case.

Injunction
An order of the court preventing or requiring action, usually in an emergency.

Judicial separation
A formal separation sanctioned by the court, which enables the courts to make orders about money and property.

Maintenance pending suit
Temporary maintenance pending finalisation of the divorce.

Matrimonial home
Any property in which a married couple live together, whether or not they own it or rent it.

Mediation
The process through which trained

independent mediators try to help a couple reach agreement about arrangements to be made for children and sometimes finances.

Parental responsibility

Where married, both parents of a child have joint parental responsibility for that child before, during and after divorce or separation. This term describes all of the rights, duties and responsibilities which, by law, a parent of a child has in relation to that child.

Periodical payments

Maintenance or alimony.

Petition

The document in which a divorce or judicial separation is applied for.

Petitioner

The person who applies for a divorce or judicial separation.

Prayer

The part of the petition that asks the court to make financial orders in favour of the petitioner.

Prohibited steps order

An order prohibiting specific steps in relation to a child, for example, a change of surname or removal from the jurisdiction.

Property adjustment order

An order that a husband or wife should transfer property to the other.

Request for directions

An application to the court for a decree nisi.

Residence order

An order dealing with the arrangements regarding with whom a child is to live.

Respondent

The other spouse, upon whom the divorce or judicial separation proceedings are served.

Separation agreement

A document setting out the terms agreed, usually before divorce proceedings are commenced.

Service

The process by which court documents are formally sent to the party to whom they are addressed (usually via their solicitor).

Specific issue order

An order determining a specific issue relating to a child; for example, an educational dispute or an issue over medical treatment.

Statement of arrangements

The form that has to be sent to the court with the petition if there are children involved, which sets out the arrangements proposed for those children when the divorce takes place. This should be agreed by the husband and wife in advance and signed by both of them if agreed.

⇨ The above information is reprinted with kind permission from Mills and Reeve. Visit www.divorce.co.uk for more information on this and other related issues.

© Mills and Reeve

Risk of divorce

Divorce risk highest within the first two years of marriage

The highest number of divorces – 10 per cent – occurred during the second year of marriage, according to figures from Divorce-Online.co.uk

Cheap and fast 'online divorces' have contributed to the 'throwaway marriage' culture, according to the internet advice site, which reports that online divorces have doubled in the past six months.

The risk of an affair stays high for the first five years of a marriage – according to the survey which polled more than 11,000 cases.

Men are the most likely to cheat and 80 per cent of infidelity divorces were instigated by spurned wives.

And almost a quarter of marriages end due to unreasonable behaviour with wives making the first move in six out of 10 cases.

Overall, a two-year separation is the most common reason for a quick divorce, at 44 per cent.

Online divorces are up 52 per cent in the past six months, according to the survey. They let couples split for as little as £65, rather than paying £2,000 for a solicitor.

With increasing concerns about the credit crunch, Mark Keenan, founder of Divorce-Online, believes the cheap prices are the main reason for the rise, as well as speed and convenience.

The figures supports official data from the Office for National Statistics (ONS) which highlighted that there were 27 divorces per 1,000 couples aged 25 to 29 in 2007.

Christine Northam of Relate, the counselling service, said: 'Younger marriages tend to be less stable. Possibly it was not strong enough to start: one of them wanted a wedding, or there was pregnancy, peer pressure.

'It all feels too much too soon and one starts looking outside the marriage.'
15 September 2008

⇨ The above information is reprinted with kind permission from Divorce Online. Visit www.divorce-online.co.uk for more information.

© Divorce Online

45 per cent of marriages will end in divorce

Taken from the Office for National Statistics publication
Population Trends 131 – Spring 2008

If current divorce rates continue around 45 per cent of marriages will end in divorce, according to a new study of the expected 'life' of marriages published today by the Office for National Statistics (ONS). It shows that almost half of these divorces will happen before married couples reach their tenth anniversary.

Once marriages survive for a decade, it is estimated that fewer than 31 per cent will end in divorce, and after 20 years, the proportion ending in divorce falls to almost 15 per cent

---

Assuming that divorce rates and death rates remain unchanged from 2005, around 10 per cent of married couples will celebrate their 60th or diamond wedding anniversary, with 45 per cent of marriages ending because of divorce and 45 per cent ending due to death.

The study, published today in the Spring issue of *Population Trends*, shows that the risk of divorce or death varies according to the duration of marriage. Once marriages survive for a decade, it is estimated that fewer than 31 per cent will end in divorce, and after 20 years, the proportion ending in divorce falls to almost 15 per cent. For marriages that survive to longer durations, divorce is rare.

Population Trends 131 contains new and up-to-date statistics and feature articles on population and demographic topics. There is an article on the 'Proportion of marriages ending in divorce' and there are two feature articles that relate to the previously released 2006-based national population projections:

⇨ The 2006-based national population projections for the UK and constituent countries.

⇨ Fertility assumptions for the 2006-based national population projections.

Other key findings from the article 'Proportion of marriages ending in divorce' include:

⇨ The proportion of marriages ending in divorce by the 50th anniversary increased from 34 per cent in 1979/80 to 37 per cent in 1987, 41 per cent in 1993/94 and 45 per cent in 2005.

⇨ Comparing 1993/94 and 2005, there is little difference in the proportion of marriages ending in divorce following 20 years of marriage. However, the 2005 analysis shows that probability of divorce is increasing for marriage durations of 30 and 40 years.

⇨ The proportion of marriages ending in divorce varies with previous marital status. Those who have been previously divorced have higher proportions of marriages ending in divorce than those who marry for the first time or those who remarry following the death of a previous spouse.

⇨ Age at marriage also influences the likelihood of divorce. Those who marry younger have higher proportions of marriages ending in divorce.

⇨ The proportion of marriages ending in divorce has stopped increasing for more recent generations of married couples. In previous analyses a rise was seen between successive marriage generations.

27 March 2008

⇨ The above information is reprinted with kind permission from the Office for National Statistics. Visit www.statistics.gov.uk for more information.

Caught in the crossfire

Put children first in separation 'crossfire', say over 90% in new poll

One in three kids will experience parental separation, yet services don't tackle conflict and emotional support say charities – as national debate launches.

93% of the public think children should come first when parents separate, yet three-quarters say services focus on custody, contact and child maintenance but don't address managing conflict and emotional damage, according to a new ICM poll released as a national debate begins on what separating families need.

76% say children are affected by parents arguing with each other

---

With 1 in 3 children set to experience parental separation before the age of 16, the ICM poll of 1,021 people, published as Kids in the Middle – The National Debate on Support for Separating Families begins, shows:

⇨ 76% say children are affected by parents arguing with each other.

⇨ 84% say more should be done to support children when their parents are going through a separation.

⇨ 93% want more opportunities for children's voices to be heard during separations.

⇨ 75% say services tend to focus on practical issues such as housing, child maintenance, contact and custody but don't address emotional support for children.

⇨ 93% say children should be a priority when parents are managing a separation.

The national debate, Kids in the Middle, backed by Relate, Families Need Fathers, One Parent Families | Gingerbread, and the Fatherhood Institute will take testimonies and evidence from parents, young people from separated families, professionals and politicians before reporting their findings and recommendations to government in the autumn.

Claire Tyler, Chief Executive of Relate, said:

'Up to 200,000 couples separate each year. Some parents manage separation reasonably amicably. But we know that if this does not happen, children in the middle of tension and disputes between separating parents can suffer a range of health, social and educational problems.

'But we have a system that seems to be in denial. Services deal with the practical issues such as money, but there is little or no support for children and families to manage the fallout from conflict. This must change.

'That's why we're launching a national debate and reporting to government how families can be better supported through separation to provide benefits which will be felt by children today and the families they raise in the future.'

The Kids in the Middle national on-line survey and debate begins today and is seeking responses and views from anyone who has experience of separating families. It can be accessed through the following websites: www.dad.info; www.relate.org.uk; www.fnf.org.uk; www.oneparentfamilies.org.uk; www.fatherhoodinstitute.org.uk

Deidre Sanders, 'Dear Deidre' of The Sun newspaper, and the nation's most famous agony aunts and uncles are also joining together to lead the debate in the media and seek their readers' views on supporting families through separation.
31 July 2008

⇨ The above information is reprinted with kind permission from Relate. Visit www.relate.org.uk for more information.

© Relate

Kids in the middle

Separated families – polling summary

Q1. *To what extent do you agree or disagree with the following statements?*

a) When parents separate, services tend to focus on practical issues such as housing, child maintenance, contact and custody but don't address emotional support for children

Net agree: 75% (strongly, 44%)

b) More should be done to support children when their parents are going through a separation

Net agree: 84% (strongly, 60%)

c) More should be done to support parents who are going through a separation

Net agree: 71% (strongly, 43%)

Q2. *How much, if at all, do you think the following affect children whose parents are going through a separation? Please use a scale of 1 to 5, where 1 means affects a lot, and 5 means does not affect at all*

a) Parents arguing with each other in front of the child

Net affects: 76% (65% affects a lot)

b) The child having to move between different houses

Net affects: 63% (46% affects a lot)

c) Losing contact with one parent

Net affects: 74% (64% affects a lot)

d) The financial cost of separation

Net affects: 54% (38% affects a lot)

Q3. *Thinking about the services offered to families during a separation. To what extent do you agree or disagree with the following statements?*

a) Children aren't encouraged to talk about their parents' separation

Net agree: 59% (strongly, 36%)

b) No direct support is given to stop/prevent conflicts between the parents when around their children

Net agree: 60% (strongly, 33%)

c) Children should be a priority when parents are managing a separation

Net agree: 93% (strongly, 80%)

Q4. *If services were to be more geared towards the needs of children during a separation, how important or unimportant do you think each of the following should be?*

a) More support to prevent arguments between parents

Net important: 85% (very important, 57%)

b) More opportunities for children's voices to be heard

Net important: 93% (very important, 70%)

c) Family counselling

Net important: 90% (very important, 60%)

d) More access for parents to practical and legal advice in sorting contact arrangements etc.

Net important: 93% (very important, 65%)

e) More access for parents to practical and legal advice in sorting out money e.g. child maintenance

Net important: 94% (very important, 69%)

4-6 July 2008 – representative sample of 1,021 adults across Great Britain

⇨ The above information is reprinted with kind permission from the Fatherhood Institute. Visit www.fatherhoodinstitute.org for more.

© Fatherhood Institute

What children might feel

Age	Signs of emotional anxiety
Babies	It can be difficult to spot signs of anxiety in babies but angry or depressed parents will pass this on to babies at a crucial time in their growth. Try to give your baby plenty of cuddles, smiles and good eye contact.
2 to 5	Children may display anger and sadness. There may be increased tearfulness. Boys may become restless and withdraw or become disruptive. Girls often try to take care of parents and become 'little adults'. Children of this age also show regressive behaviour like bedwetting.
6 to 8	Children will often display sadness through increased tearfulness. Family separation can leave them feeling rejected and unloved. You may notice a drop in school performance or hear that they have become disruptive in class. Boys will very often miss their fathers intensely.
9 to 11	Children of this age will very often become angry, especially towards the parent that they think is responsible for the separation. They often feel frightened and want nothing more than for you to get back together again. You may notice a drop in school performance and sometimes an increase in headaches, sickness or nightmares.
Older	Some children in this age group, especially older ones, may become more independent and focus their energies outside the family and on their future. This can be a good thing. There is a danger that, whilst parents are dealing with the ending of their relationship, children of this age may drift away from the family unit and seek approval with their peers. This can lead to risky behaviour such as drinking, drug taking, inappropriate sexual activity and crime.

It can be quite difficult to spot signs of emotional stress and anxiety in children. This is because children see that you are distressed and don't want to make things worse for you. However, it's very important that you spot any changes in behaviour and help your children deal with these feelings. Children of all ages often feel:

⇨ confused
⇨ frightened
⇨ sad
⇨ hurt
⇨ let down
⇨ angry
⇨ guilty.

Children very often feel responsible for their parents' separation; this can lead to feelings of guilt as well as a belief that they can bring you back together. They will be aware of the pain around the separation of your adult relationship and may well bury their own feelings so as not to make you feel worse. Any conflict that occurs during your separation will have a particularly unsettling effect on them.

Source: separatedfamilies.info

The emotional cost of parental separation

Children who come from separated families where there is conflict are less likely to want children of their own, according to a survey

The true emotional cost of parental separation emerged in a report which revealed children's scars linger long after the event and can affect their school performance.

It also emerged that kids who see their parents break up are more likely not to want children of their own in the future.

Researchers also found children whose mum and dad split are more likely to struggle to find true happiness in their own lives.

Karen Woodall, Director for The Centre for Separated Families, which commissioned the 'Happiness, hopes and wellbeing' study of 1,000 children under the age of 15, said:

'We recognise that there are many situations where one parent is left alone to provide everything that children need, however, we also recognise that the children who do best after family separation are those that have a strong and positive input from both parents.

'Both parents need to identify their children's needs and work out the best way to contribute to providing for them.'

The study was carried out to coincide with the Best Practice in Supporting Separated Families Conference which is being held in London with contributions from the new Child Maintenance Commissioner Stephen Geraghty, Anthony Douglas, CEO of Cafcass and the Rt Hon Iain Duncan Smith MP.

It asked children from separated and settled households to gauge their personal happiness on a scale of one to ten.

Those from families where mum and dad now live apart scored significantly lower than those from settled homes.

And only three-quarters said their relationships with their parents were good, while 93 per cent of children whose parents were still together said the same thing.

It also emerged that one in four kids from a separated family don't consider themselves to be happy compared to only one in ten from a stable home.

Ms Woodall continued:

'The absence of conflict is key to children's wellbeing and we know that parents need help to resolve difficult issues and build new cooperative relationships.'

The Best Practice in Support to Separated Families Conference brings together experts to find new ways to support separated families to bring about better outcomes for children.

Seminars will consider all the important issues, child maintenance, parenting arrangements and how to help children to enjoy relationships with both of their parents.

Stephen Geraghty, the Commissioner for Child Maintenance, said:

'The Commission has been tasked with offering information and support on the different child maintenance options available to parents. This conference will allow us to talk about the work of the Commission and listen to key stakeholders working in the field of family separation.'

Anthony Douglas, Chief Executive of Cafcass, said:

'Services like therapeutic mediation, child counselling, family group conferencing and parenting information classes, can help parents and children to move on together – rather than parents moving on and children left emotionally stranded.'

The Centre for Separated Families helps parents to build cooperative relationships so that they can help their children to adjust to the change.

Ms Woodall concluded:

'It is a sad fact that children are affected in many different ways when their parents decide to separate. We want to make things easier for children and easier for parents too.

'We know that children wish their parents would stay together and we also know that for many parents that just isn't possible. But by helping parents to understand how their children feel we can help them to stop fighting and start talking again which is crucial if children are going to adapt well.'

The study also revealed that 14 per cent of kids wanted their parents to live together even if they didn't get on that well.

15 October 2008

⇨ The above information is reprinted with kind permission from the Centre for Separated Families. Visit www.separatedfamilies.info for more information.

Happiness, hopes and wellbeing

A survey of children's views on parental relationships

Survey details

The survey asked 1,000 children living in households to tell us whether their parents are:

a) Married or living together;
b) Separated or divorced with a good or friendly relationship;
c) Separated or divorced with a bad or unfriendly relationship.

A series of 25 questions about perceptions of happiness, hopes for the future and perceptions of wellbeing were then put to the children and the results were analysed according to the three different categories.

Sample questions and responses

We asked children to rate themselves on a scale of one to ten:

How happy are you?

Children who rated themselves the happiest were those living with both parents; statistically almost two and a half times happier than children living in separated or divorced households whose parents maintained a bad or unfriendly relationship.

Over a quarter of children living with separated or divorced parents who maintained good or friendly relationships considered themselves to be happy compared to a fifth of children living in households with divorced or separated parents who had a bad or unfriendly relationship.

We asked children to tell us:

How close are you to your parents?

Children living with both parents and children living with divorced or separated parents who have good relationships considered themselves closer to their parents.

Almost one-quarter of children living with divorced or separated parents with bad relationships revealed they were not close to their parents.

We asked children to tell us about their home life.

Over 90% of children living with both parents and similarly those children living with separated parents who maintained healthy relationships said they were happy.

However, 1 in 5 children living with divorced or separated parents who have bad relationships disclosed they were unhappy with their home life and felt that this would mean they were less likely to achieve in life.

We asked children:

Are you happy with your achievements at school or college?

Children who were happiest with their school/college/work were those living with both parents or separated parents who had a good relationship.

We asked children about their perception of wellbeing in relation to marriage or living together:

Do you feel that children whose parents are married or living together get a better start in life than those whose parents are divorced or separated?

Children living with divorced or separated parents with good relationships feel that they had been given a far greater start in life than those living with divorced or separated parents with bad relationships.

Whilst seventy per cent of children whose parents were divorced or separated with a bad or unfriendly relationship felt that children whose parents are married or living together get a better start in life.

We then asked children to consider questions about their own future as parents. We asked:

Would you like to have children when you are older?

Children whose parents were divorced or separated were less likely to want to have children of their own in later life.

The survey also asked:

Do you think it is important that parents live together when they have children?

Almost all of the children whose parents were married or living together felt that it was important for parents to live together whilst children whose parents were divorced and separated but with a good or friendly relationship were less likely to feel that.

The highest proportion of children who felt it was not important were those living with divorced or separated parents with bad or unfriendly relationships.

We asked about family and separation and whether this had affected children's lives.

Nearly three-quarters of the children living with divorced or separated parents with bad or unfriendly relationships recognised that their lives had been affected in ways that included not seeing one of their parents as much as they would like, losing touch with grandparents, aunts and uncles and having to witness their parents' arguments.

Our final question to children was:

If your parents were not getting along, would you prefer them to separate or continue to live together?

Overwhelmingly, all children said that they would prefer their parents to stay together rather than separate, even if they were not getting on well together.

The poll was undertaken by One Poll in October 2008.

⇨ The above information is reprinted with kind permission from the Centre for Separated Families. Visit www.separatedfamilies.info for more information.

© *Centre for Separated Families*

Experiences of children in divorce proceedings

Statistics taken from the NSPCC report 'Your shout too! A survey of the views of children and young people involved in court proceedings when their parents divorce or separate'.

Extent to which young people felt involved, and could influence the outcome (in the court proceedings).

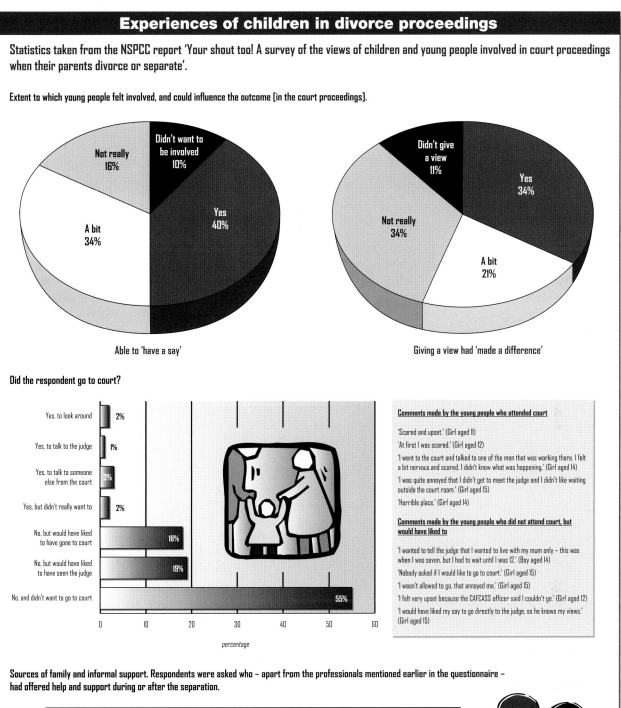

Able to 'have a say'

- Didn't want to be involved 10%
- Yes 40%
- A bit 34%
- Not really 16%

Giving a view had 'made a difference'

- Didn't give a view 11%
- Yes 34%
- A bit 21%
- Not really 34%

Did the respondent go to court?

	percentage
Yes, to look around	2%
Yes, to talk to the judge	1%
Yes, to talk to someone else from the court	3%
Yes, but didn't really want to	2%
No, but would have liked to have gone to court	18%
No, but would have liked to have seen the judge	19%
No, and didn't want to go to court	55%

Comments made by the young people who attended court

'Scared and upset.' (Girl aged 11)

'At first I was scared.' (Girl aged 12)

'I went to the court and talked to one of the men that was working there. I felt a bit nervous and scared. I didn't know what was happening.' (Girl aged 14)

'I was quite annoyed that I didn't get to meet the judge and I didn't like waiting outside the court room.' (Girl aged 15)

'Horrible place.' (Girl aged 14)

Comments made by the young people who did not attend court, but would have liked to

'I wanted to tell the judge that I wanted to live with my mum only – this was when I was seven, but I had to wait until I was 12.' (Boy aged 14)

'Nobody asked if I would like to go to court.' (Girl aged 15)

'I wasn't allowed to go, that annoyed me.' (Girl aged 15)

'I felt very upset because the CAFCASS officer said I couldn't go.' (Girl aged 12)

'I would have liked my say to go directly to the judge, so he knows my views.' (Girl aged 15)

Sources of family and informal support. Respondents were asked who – apart from the professionals mentioned earlier in the questionnaire – had offered help and support during or after the separation.

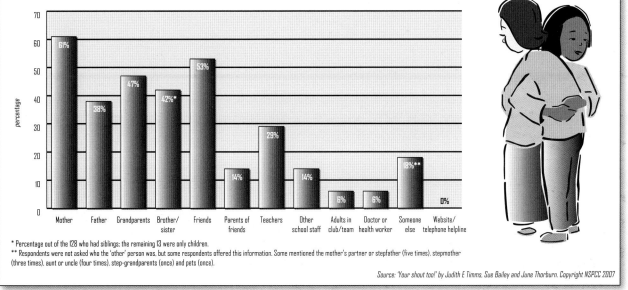

Source	Percentage
Mother	61%
Father	38%
Grandparents	47%
Brother/sister	42%*
Friends	53%
Parents of friends	14%
Teachers	29%
Other school staff	14%
Adults in club/team	6%
Doctor or health worker	6%
Someone else	18%**
Website/telephone helpline	0%

* Percentage out of the 128 who had siblings; the remaining 13 were only children.

** Respondents were not asked who the 'other' person was, but some respondents offered this information. Some mentioned the mother's partner or stepfather (five times), stepmother (three times), aunt or uncle (four times), step-grandparents (once) and pets (once).

Source: 'Your shout too!' by Judith E Timms, Sue Bailey and June Thorburn. Copyright NSPCC 2007

Divorce law and your children

Information from Divorce Aid

This period of your life is so emotionally charged that it is not unusual to forget how your children may be feeling. It is vital that any child is reassured that both parents do love him and care for him despite the marriage problems and that this parental responsibility (see below) will continue during all the stages of separation and divorce and afterwards.

> **It is vital that any child is reassured that both parents do love him and care for him despite the marriage problems**

Most parents agree

Most parents agree about the arrangements for children, although difficulties do arise frequently, especially when matters of finance are also in dispute. The law considers that these voluntary arrangements between parents are more likely to succeed in the long run than those imposed by the courts. It is therefore generally understood that the courts will not intervene unless it is in the best interests of the child. Your child, like the courts, would prefer you both to do your utmost to put him first, to see things through the eyes of your child. Mediation may be offered as an alternative to the court process and details are given below.

When filing for divorce

When filing for divorce, a Statement of Arrangements has also to be filed, giving details of the proposed arrangements for the children. If these are agreed by both of you, the court is unlikely to interfere although you can ask for the court to help at any time. If agreement has not been reached, the Judge may ask for you both to attend a hearing to see if you can agree. Mediation may again be advised. Reports could be requested and further meetings probably with the children in attendance at a CAFCASS (court welfare) office or at home. See below for further details. This is best discussed with your solicitor.

What does the law say?

The Children Act 1989 says that the child's welfare is the most important consideration. The old word 'access' has been replaced by contact. This can refer to contact by letter, phone and actual visits. 'Custody' has been replaced by residence. The Act describes parental responsibility rather than parents' rights. If you were married when the child was born, both of you will have parental responsibility for the child. A father who was not married to the child's mother when the child was born, will not automatically have parental responsibility for that child. But can acquire it by agreement with the child's mother or by applying to the court. He can also acquire it by marrying the child's mother after the birth.

Parental responsibility

Parental responsibility means that you are both responsible for the following but this list is by no means complete:
⇨ protecting and maintaining your child;
⇨ naming the child;
⇨ choosing the school;
⇨ making sure he goes to school from age 5 to 16;
⇨ making sure they receive medical treatment;
⇨ appointing a guardian to act after death;
⇨ applying for a passport;
⇨ representing the child;
⇨ deciding where he is to live;
⇨ choosing the child's religion etc.

What about money?

A parent has financial responsibility for the child until he reaches the age of 17 or leaves full-time education, whichever is the later. There is no 'clean break' (an end to providing

financial support) between parents and children. This is the law. A child's father (or mother) is obliged to pay for this support whether or not there is any contact. The two issues are entirely separate but in reality disagreements about maintenance sometimes lead to problems with contact. On the other hand, a father who has regular contact is more likely to pay maintenance on a regular basis. Try to keep these two issues separate and discuss them at separate times. For details about obtaining financial support for your child, please refer to the Financial section on the Divorce Aid website (www.divorceaid.co.uk).

Will continued abuse affect the children?

If violence or psychological abuse caused your separation, this behaviour may continue and even get worse. Controlling behaviour and abuse are also likely to affect the child at contact times and afterwards. Your physical and mental safety is crucial for your child's wellbeing.

Can we avoid going to court about the children?

If under normal circumstances, you are unable to agree on contact arrangements, to put your children first, to compromise, to maintain some stability, to allow your child to continue to love both parents, mediation could be the best option. This is so much better than 'going to court' which may be costly, lengthy and distressing to all concerned.

What is mediation?

A mediator is a trained professional who listens to both parents' wishes and concerns and tries to help you both come to some arrangement about contact. (Mediation is also used in disputes regarding where the child should live, 'residence', and other issues such as finances and property. Ask your solicitor or mediator if you are eligible for funding. For more details, see the Legal section on the Divorce Aid website: www.divorceaid. co.uk)

Again, if you are in fear of violence, this is not the course for you to take.

You can either request a mediator through your solicitor or contact

NFM at www.nfm.org.uk/
Write to them at:
National Family Mediation
9 Tavistock Place
London WC1 9SN
Tel: 0207 383 5993
In Scotland:
Family Mediation Scotland
127 Rose Street,
South Lane,
Edinburgh
EH2 4BB
Tel: 0131 226 4507

They should be able to put you in contact with a local mediator. Even if this does not seem feasible at the moment, you can bear this in mind for later when your emotions are more settled. Always remember to talk to your child. What does she want? Are you making her unhappy? Are you giving her your best? Put yourself in her shoes.

What if mediation and talking fail?

If mediation and all other communication fail, including talking to your child and listening to him, you may have to consider court action but this will not give you an instant solution.

Again, the courts base their decisions on the Children Act which emphasises the welfare of the child. The court will only make an order if it is in the best interests of the child.

It is not your 'access' to the child that is paramount; it is what is best for the child.

The courts consider the following factors:

⇨ the child's feelings and wishes, depending on his age and understanding;
⇨ the physical, emotional and educational needs of the child;
⇨ the likely effect of any changes in his circumstances;
⇨ the age, sex and background and any characteristics which the Court considers relevant;
⇨ any harm which the child may have suffered or is at risk of suffering;
⇨ how capable each of the parents is of meeting the child's needs (this may include other involved people).

You will need a solicitor

This legal process requires a family

law solicitor. It may become costly unless you are able to receive funding from the Community Legal Service (Legal aid). (Details about how to find a family solicitor and other information are in the Legal section on the Divorce Aid website: www. divorceaid.co.uk. Suggested books are in the Books section. Have you read Children/Teenagers/Parents sections? These may help you both come to some understanding and agreement. If you haven't already read through Emotions and Health sections, these may help you to understand each other's position and concerns.) Always look for common ground and try to see things through the eyes of a child.

What if we can't agree where the child should live?

It may be worth remembering that most families do not involve the courts and the courts generally consider that it is the right of each child to have a relationship with both parents.

It is rare for families to disagree about where a child will live – this is referred to as Residence. The court would consider, amongst other things, the following:
⇨ the working parent who must arrange childcare will not be preferred to the parent at home – continuation of the status quo;
⇨ maintenance of family contacts;
⇨ 'normal' family life;
⇨ permanence and stability;
⇨ the child's wishes when able to express these in a mature and balanced way;
⇨ adequate mothering especially for young children;
⇨ avoiding separating siblings.

What else can the courts do?

The courts can also deal with specific issues as well as contact and residence orders.

A 'Specific Issue Order' could be sought to decide where a child will go to school or to decide on medical treatment. There is also a 'Prohibited Steps Order' which can stop something from happening. One example would be to stop one parent from taking the child abroad. A solicitor's advice should be sought. Please contact us.

What happens at court?

This will involve CAFCASS, the Children and Family Court Advisory and Support Service for England and Wales. It is a group of professionals, answerable to the Lord Chancellor, who provide advice to the courts about the wellbeing of children and their families. You are both usually requested to attend a meeting with the Judge four to ten weeks after applying for a court order. Your solicitors generally attend too.

The Children Act 1989 says that the child's welfare is the most important consideration

---

CAFCASS and the court welfare report

A CAFCASS officer is normally in attendance too but practice varies from court to court. The purpose of this meeting is for the court to ascertain whether there is any chance of you coming to an agreement. If not, it is normal practice for the Judge to request a CAFCASS (court welfare) report. This can be a lengthy document and is only drawn up after he meets the parents together or individually and he meets with the child/children either on their own or/and with a parent/s.

He can also check whether their schools have any concerns. He can also check with doctors, Social Services, the police etc.; visits may also be arranged at home. Although you will be dealing with professional people, this can be a very emotional and traumatic time.

Try to agree yourselves

Throughout the whole process, you will be encouraged to come to an agreement that is in the best interests of the child. The hearing would then be arranged for perhaps three to six months later if you haven't already found a solution and the Judge would then deliver his decision which is often in agreement with the welfare report's recommendations. He could also delay his decision for a further

period of time and order another hearing in the hope of agreement. An appeal against the decision could also be considered. This could turn out to be a costly and lengthy procedure which could add to the stresses of the divorce and diminish your ability to co-operate as responsible parents.

What is international parental child abduction?

This is the removal or retention of a child across an international border by one parent (or person who has parental responsibility), which is either in contravention of a court order or without the consent of the other parent (or person who has parental responsibility).

Is it a criminal offence for one parent to abduct a child?

In most circumstances, YES!

reunite is the leading UK charity specialising in international parental child abduction

reunite provides advice, information and support to parents, family members and guardians who have had a child abducted or who fear child abduction. They also provide advice to parents who may have abducted their child as well as advising on international contact issues. Please kindly mention Divorce Aid to them.

For further details please see their website at www.reunite.org or call their advice line on 0116 2556 234. From abroad, call +44 116 2556 234

Write to them at:
P.O. Box 7124
Leicester
LE1 7XX
United Kingdom

Please try to remember this

You should both work towards establishing a parenting agreement that will benefit your child. This is not about any other disagreement you may have. Although you may think that 'fighting' over your child shows your child how much you love him, this is not the case. A child, like the courts, will be waiting for you to co-operate together. Arrangements which are agreed between you are more likely to be honoured.

Time is a healer; things will get better if you try to stop hurting each other. Try to do something constructive for your spouse, something that could build trust and co-operation. Stand back and reflect. Remember to see everything through the eyes of your child.

⇨ The above information is re-printed with kind permission from Divorce Aid. Visit www.divorceaid.co.uk for more information.
© Divorce Aid

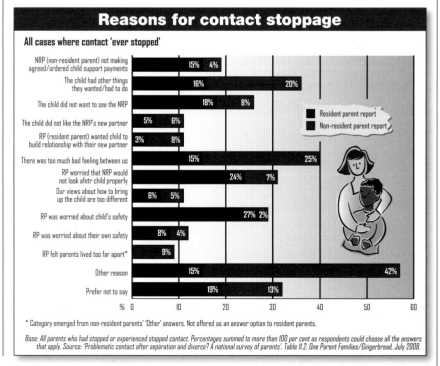

Reasons for contact stoppage

All cases where contact 'ever stopped'

* Category emerged from non-resident parents' 'Other' answers. Not offered as an answer option to resident parents.

Base: All parents who had stopped or experienced stopped contact. Percentages summed to more than 100 per cent as respondents could choose all the answers that apply. Source: 'Problematic contact after separation and divorce? A national survey of parents'. Table II.2. One Parent Families/Gingerbread, July 2008.

Contact patterns after separation and divorce

An extract from *Problematic contact after separation and divorce? A national survey of parents*

An unexpectedly high proportion of parents reported that they shared care more or less equally with the other parent.

⇨ Twelve per cent of all those responding to the survey said they had shared care arrangements.

⇨ Even if allowance is made for the disproportionately low numbers of non-resident parents taking part in the survey, this still works out at 9 per cent. If one regards all parents with shared care as resident parents, then 17 per cent of resident parents are sharing care more or less equally.

---

71 per cent of resident parents, including those with shared care, said that their child had direct contact with the other parent

---

The majority of children have face-to-face contact with their non-resident parent although a substantial minority do not, of whom most have never had contact since their parents separated.

⇨ Across the whole sample, 71 per cent of resident parents, including those with shared care, said that their child had direct contact with the other parent.

⇨ If the shared-care parents are excluded, 65 per cent of resident parents, and 85 per cent of non-resident parents reported some contact.

⇨ Of the resident parents who said there was no contact at the moment, most said there had either been no contact since the parental relationship ended (63

per cent) or that the father was not aware of the child's existence (6 per cent).

⇨ The small number of non-resident parents without current contact taking part in the study were more likely to report there had been some contact in the past but the majority said there had not (54 per cent of 24).

Where there is contact, the most common pattern is weekly, but there is wide variation. The frequencies reported by resident and non-resident parents were very similar.

⇨ Forty-two per cent of resident and 45 per cent of non-resident parents reported seeing their child at least once a week, although not nearly every day.

⇨ Ten per cent of resident and 9 per cent of non-resident parents said there was contact daily or almost daily.

⇨ Sixty-nine per cent of resident and 68 per cent of non-resident parents reported at least fortnightly contact.

⇨ Eleven per cent of resident and 9 per cent of non-resident

parents said contact was less than fortnightly but at least once a month.

⇨ Twenty-one per cent of resident and 23 per cent of non-resident parents said contact took place less often than monthly, including some (5 per cent resident; 13 per cent non-resident) who said it was only once or twice a year.

⇨ If the parents who reported shared care are included as resident parents the data indicates that 76 per cent of children were having at least fortnightly contact and 64 per cent weekly.

Where there is contact it will typically include overnight stays, usually at least monthly.

⇨ Sixty-five per cent of resident and 79 per cent of non-resident parents whose child had contact (but were not sharing care) said this included overnight stays.

⇨ Where there were overnight stays 31 per cent of resident and 39 per cent of non-resident parents said this occurred at least once a week with 72 per cent and 73 per cent respectively saying it was at least once a month.

⇨ Thirteen per cent of resident and 12 per cent of non-resident parents said overnight stays only happened in the holidays or a few times a year.

⇨ Fourteen per cent and 16 per cent said it only happened once or twice a year.

⇨ If the parents who reported shared care are included, then 55 per cent of children with contact were having overnight stays at least once a week, and 83 per cent at least once a month.

Children who have overnight contact tend to have more contact in the holidays, but those with only visiting contact typically do not.

⇨ Fifty-three per cent of resident and 73 per cent of non-resident parents whose child had overnight contact said there was more contact in the holidays. Extra contact in the holidays was even more likely where overnight contact usually took place at least weekly (57 per cent resident parent; 92 per cent non-resident parent).

⇨ Where contact was on a visiting basis only 10 per cent of resident and 19 per cent of non-resident parents said it was more frequent in the holidays and 4 per cent of resident and 34 per cent of non-resident parents said it actually decreased.

Contact is rarely stable over time and is more likely to reduce than increase.

⇨ Where there has ever been contact only 32 per cent of resident and 28 per cent of non-resident parents who had been separated for more than a year said that the amount of contact had stayed the same.

⇨ Fifty-one per cent of resident parents and 42 per cent of non-resident parents said that contact had reduced or stopped; only 14 per cent and 26 per cent, respectively, said that it had increased, with the remainder saying either that it had been variable or being unable to answer.

⇨ Even where contact was ongoing only 40 per cent of resident and 37 per cent of non-resident parents said the amount of contact had stayed the same; while 38 per cent and 31 per cent said it had reduced and only 17 per cent and 29 per cent said it had increased.

⇨ Some children appear to have had quite high levels of contact throughout (64 per cent of resident and 63 per cent of non-resident parents who said contact had stayed the same reported contact at least weekly).

⇨ In contrast, 10 per cent of resident and 13 per cent of non-resident parents who said contact had stayed the same reported that contact took place less than once a month.

July 2008

⇨ The above information is reprinted with kind permission from One Parent Families | Gingerbread and is an extract from their report *Problematic contact after separation and divorce? A national survey of parents.* Visit www.oneparentfamilies.org.uk for more information.

© *One Parent Families | Gingerbread*

Mediation and you

Mediation helps those involved in family breakdown to communicate better with one another and reach their own decisions about all or some of the issues arising from separation or divorce – children, property and finance

Mediation is about directly negotiating your own decisions with the help of a third party. It is an alternative to solicitors negotiating for you or having decisions made for you by the courts. Entering mediation is always voluntary.

How does it work?

A trained mediator will meet with you both for a series of sessions in which you will be helped to:

⇨ Identify all the matters you wish to consider

⇨ Collect the necessary information.

⇨ Talk about the choices open to you.

⇨ Negotiate with each other to reach decisions that are acceptable to you both.

⇨ Discuss how you can consult your children appropriately about arrangements.

What does the mediator do?

The mediator's job is to act as an impartial third party and manage the process, helping you to exchange information, ideas and feelings constructively and ensuring that you make informed decisions. The mediator has no power to impose a settlement – responsibility for all decisions remains with yourselves since you know better than anyone else what is right for your family. The mediator will not advise you about the best option either for your children or your financial affairs, nor can the mediator protect your individual interest.

Will I still need a solicitor?

YES! You will need a solicitor to advise

you on the personal consequences for you of your proposals. You will be encouraged to engage a solicitor whom you can consult during the mediation process. At the end of mediation your solicitor will be able to advise you about your proposals and translate them into a legally binding form.

Will we have anything in writing?

At the end of mediation you will usually have achieved a written summary of the proposals you have reached. This is not a legally binding document and you will need legal advice about it especially if you have reached agreement on financial and property issues.

Mediation is about directly negotiating your own decisions with the help of a third party. It is an alternative to solicitors negotiating for you or having decisions made for you by the courts

---

How much will it cost?

Each Service has their own scale of charges. They will also be able to advise you if you are eligible for legally aided mediation, which is free.

Is mediation suitable for everybody?

Sometimes mediation is not the best way for you to resolve your problems. You will have a chance to discuss this in more detail at your first individual meeting with the mediator.

Is mediation confidential?

Firstly mediation is confidential and courts are also likely to regard the discussions as privileged.

Confidentiality – The Service will not voluntarily disclose to outsiders any information obtained in the course of your discussions without first obtaining your permission (unless it appears there is a risk of significant harm to adult or child).

Privilege – What you say during mediation cannot be used later in court as evidence. But facts disclosed during mediation are regarded as open information and although strictly confidential may be used subsequently in court.

Will the mediator talk to the children?

In mediation you are regarded as the experts on your children and will have valuable knowledge and information about their needs, wishes and views. However, there may be times when you both would like the mediator to consult directly with the children about your plans. In those circumstances children would be asked for their specific comments and views on your joint proposals, without having to take sides in any difference of opinion between their parents.

Such a meeting needs careful planning and is confidential in so far as the mediator and children agree what the mediator will say to the parents after the meeting.

What are the benefits of mediation?

Research conducted by the Joseph Rowntree Foundation with Newcastle University identified that three years later couples felt that mediation had helped them to:

⇨ End the marital relationship amicably.
⇨ Reduce conflict.
⇨ Maintain good relationships with their ex-spouses.
⇨ Carry less bitterness and resentment into their post-divorce lives.
⇨ Be more content with existing child care arrangements and less likely to have disagreement about child contact.
⇨ Be able to reach agreement that had survived the test of time.
⇨ Be glad they had used mediation.
Source: Family Mediation

⇨ The above information is reprinted with kind permission from Divorce Online. Visit www.divorce-online.co.uk for more information.
© *Divorce Online*

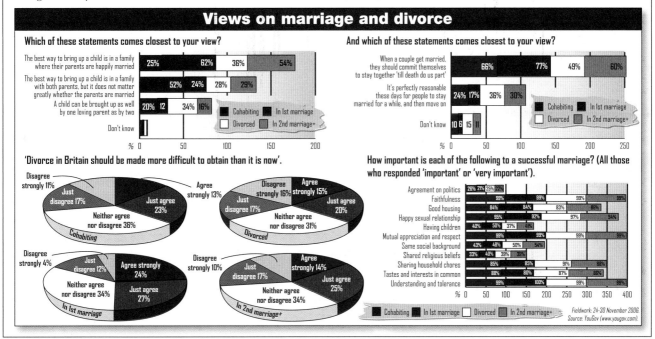

Views on marriage and divorce

Which of these statements comes closest to your view?

The best way to bring up a child is in a family where their parents are happily married — 25% | 62% | 36% | 54%
The best way to bring up a child is in a family with both parents, but it does not matter greatly whether the parents are married — 52% | 24% | 28% | 29%
A child can be brought up as well by one loving parent as by two — 20% | 12 | 34% | 16%
Don't know

Legend: Cohabiting | In 1st marriage | Divorced | In 2nd marriage+

And which of these statements comes closest to your view?

When a couple get married, they should commit themselves to stay together 'till death do us part' — 66% | 77% | 49% | 60%
It's perfectly reasonable these days for people to stay married for a while, and then move on — 24% | 17% | 36% | 30%
Don't know — 10 | 6 | 15 | 11

Legend: Cohabiting | In 1st marriage | Divorced | In 2nd marriage+

'Divorce in Britain should be made more difficult to obtain than it is now'.

Cohabiting: Disagree strongly 11% | Just disagree 17% | Neither agree nor disagree 36% | Just agree 23% | Agree strongly 13%

Divorced: Disagree strongly 16% | Just disagree 17% | Neither agree nor disagree 31% | Just agree 20% | Agree strongly 15%

In 1st marriage: Disagree strongly 4% | Just disagree 12% | Neither agree nor disagree 34% | Just agree 27% | Agree strongly 24%

In 2nd marriage+: Disagree strongly 10% | Just disagree 17% | Neither agree nor disagree 34% | Just agree 25% | Agree strongly 14%

How important is each of the following to a successful marriage? (All those who responded 'important' or 'very important').

	Cohabiting	In 1st marriage	Divorced	In 2nd marriage+
Agreement on politics	26%	21%	25%	22%
Faithfulness	99%	99%	99%	99%
Good housing	84%	84%	83%	86%
Happy sexual relationship	95%	92%	97%	94%
Having children	40%	50%	37%	41%
Mutual appreciation and respect	99%	99%	99%	99%
Same social background	43%	48%	50%	54%
Shared religious beliefs	33%	40%	39%	38%
Sharing household chores	85%	85%	91%	88%
Tastes and interests in common	88%	80%	87%	86%
Understanding and tolerance	99%	100%	99%	99%

Fieldwork: 24-30 November 2006.
Source: YouGov (www.yougov.com).

⇨ Getting married is still popular in Britain, with most people marrying at some point in their lives. Choosing to share your life with a partner is still the most common lifestyle choice. 57% of British households consisted of a married or cohabiting heterosexual couple in 2006. (page 1)

⇨ Analysis of marriage expectations suggests that cohabiting partners are less likely to marry each other once they have had a baby: a larger proportion of women with children than childless women (60% compared with 45%) never wish to marry their present partner, and the results are similar for men (66% compared with 47%). (page 2)

⇨ In 2006 there were 236,980 weddings in England and Wales, of which 39 per cent were remarriages for one or both parties. (page 4)

⇨ Marriage rates in England and Wales have fallen to the lowest level since records began, according to provisional figures for 2006 released by the ONS. (page 6)

⇨ Millions of Brits are stuck in unhappy marriages but will not walk away for fear of financial or emotional hardship, a report from international law firm Seddons has revealed. The study revealed 59 per cent of women would end their marriage today if their future financial security was assured. (page 7)

⇨ Despite a campaign to raise awareness, half of people (51%) still believe (wrongly) that there is such a thing as 'common-law marriage' which gives cohabitants the same rights as married couples. (page 12)

⇨ The number of cohabiting couple families in the UK increased by 65 per cent between 1996 and 2006 and the number of married couple families fell by 4 per cent, according to a report published this week by a team of researchers from the Office of National Statistics (ONS), LSE and Warwick University. (page 15)

⇨ There is growing concern thousands of British girls are being taken out of schools and forced into marriages after new figures hinted the problem was far worse than previously thought. A study by the Home Office found there were more than 300 inquiries in the town of Luton in one year and the issue is likely to be widespread across the country. (page 20)

⇨ To get a divorce in England and Wales, you need to show that you have been married for more than a year and that the marriage has broken down. (page 21)

⇨ In 2007 the provisional divorce rate in England and Wales fell to 11.9 divorcing people per 1,000 married population compared with the 2006 figure of 12.2. The divorce rate is at its lowest level since 1981. (page 25)

⇨ The highest number of divorces – 10 per cent – occurred during the second year of marriage, according to figures from Divorce-Online.co.uk. (page 27)

⇨ If current divorce rates continue around 45 per cent of marriages will end in divorce, according to a new study of the expected 'life' of marriages published today by the Office for National Statistics (ONS). It shows that almost half of these divorces will happen before married couples reach their tenth anniversary. (page 28)

⇨ 93% of the public think children should come first when parents separate, yet three-quarters say services focus on custody, contact and child maintenance but don't address managing conflict and emotional damage, according to a new ICM poll. (page 29)

⇨ It has emerged that kids who see their parents break up are more likely not to want children of their own in the future. Researchers also found children whose mum and dad split are more likely to struggle to find true happiness in their own lives. (page 31)

⇨ In a survey, children were asked to rate themselves on a scale of one to ten. When asked the question 'How happy are you?', children who rated themselves the happiest were those living with both parents; statistically almost two and a half times happier than children living in separated or divorced households whose parents maintained a bad or unfriendly relationship. (page 32)

⇨ The Children Act 1989 says that the child's welfare is the most important consideration during divorce proceedings. (page 34)

⇨ 71 per cent of resident parents, including those with shared care, said that their child had direct contact with the other parent. (page 37)

⇨ Contact is rarely stable over time and is more likely to reduce than increase. Where there has ever been contact, only 32 per cent of resident and 28 per cent of non-resident parents who had been separated for more than a year said that the amount of contact had stayed the same. (page 38)

⇨ 13% of cohabiting couples surveyed agreed strongly with the statement: 'Divorce in Britain should be made more difficult to obtain than it is now', compared with 24% of people in their first marriage, 14% of those in their second or subsequent marriage and 15% of those who were divorced. (page 39)

GLOSSARY

Adultery
A married individual who commits adultery has a sexual relationship with someone other than their spouse, usually without their spouse's knowledge. This can be given as grounds for divorce.

Arranged marriage
In an arranged marriage, the families take the leading role in choosing a marriage partner for their offspring. Both parties involved consent to this and have the right to reject a marriage partner they find objectionable. An arranged marriage is therefore not the same as a forced marriage. Arranged marriages are relatively common among some cultures, nationalities and religious faiths.

Civil partnership
The Civil Partnership Act 2004 gave same-sex couples choosing to enter a civil partnership the same rights and responsibilities as spouses in a civil marriage. When couples in a civil partnership decide to legally end their relationship, it is called dissolution (rather than divorce).

Cohabitation
Couples who cohabit live together, but are not married or in a civil partnership.

Common-law marriage
Half of adults still believe in a 'common-law marriage', whereby couples who have been living together for a long period of time are entitled to the same rights as married couples. In reality, common-law marriage does not exist.

Contact
Replacing the old word 'access', 'contact' in terms of divorce refers to the contact between a child and their non-resident parent, as agreed by the court during the divorce proceedings.

Divorce
The legal process leading to the end of a marriage.

Forced marriage
Unlike an arranged marriage, in a forced marriage one or more of the participants enters into the marriage only through coercion or force. Forced marriage is illegal in the UK and classed as a form of domestic violence.

Marriage
Marriage is the legal union of a couple. It may also have religious and social significance to the couple. It is usually marked with a ceremony (wedding) to celebrate the couple's union.

Mediation
Mediation is a process designed to resolve disputes among divorcing couples. A trained mediator will help the couple to discuss any issues arising from their divorce and resolve them in the best way possible. It is not the same as marriage guidance counselling, as its purpose is not to help the couple repair their relationship; it simply aims to make the divorce process as painless as possible for those involved.

Separation
This occurs when a couple have acknowledged the failure of their marriage and no longer live together, but have not yet obtained a divorce. Some separated couples may choose not to start divorce proceedings right away, or at all.

Stepfamily
A stepfamily is a family an individual becomes a part of when a parent marries or remarries someone who already has a family from a previous relationship. Stepfamily members are not blood relatives, but are connected as a family through the marriage of their parents.

INDEX

Additional Resources

Other Issues *titles*

If you are interested in researching further some of the issues raised in *Marriage and Cohabitation*, you may like to read the following titles in the **Issues** series:

⇨ Vol. 155 *Domestic Abuse* (ISBN 978 1 86168 442 4)

⇨ Vol. 154 *The Gender Gap* (ISBN 978 1 86168 441 7)

⇨ Vol. 153 *Sexual Orientation and Society* (ISBN 978 1 86168 440 0)

⇨ Vol. 133 *Teen Pregnancy and Lone Parents* (ISBN 978 1 86168 379 3)

⇨ Vol. 132 *Child Abuse* (ISBN 978 1 86168 378 6)

⇨ Vol. 130 *Homelessness* (ISBN 978 1 86168 376 2)

⇨ Vol. 126 *The Abortion Debate* (ISBN 978 1 86168 365 6)

⇨ Vol. 124 *Parenting Issues* (ISBN 978 1 86168 363 2)

For more information about these titles, visit our website at www.independence.co.uk/publicationslist

Useful organisations

You may find the websites of the following organisations useful for further research:

⇨ **Care for the Family:** www.careforthefamily.org.uk

⇨ **Centre for Separated Families:** www.separatedfamilies.info

⇨ **Divorce Aid:** www.divorceaid.co.uk

⇨ **Divorce Online:** www.divorce-online.co.uk

⇨ **Family and Parenting Institute:** www.familyandparenting.org

⇨ **Fatherhood Institute:** www.fatherhoodinstitute.org

⇨ **Forced Marriage Unit:** www.fco.gov.uk/forcedmarriage

⇨ **London School of Economics and Political Science:** www.lse.ac.uk

⇨ **Mills and Reeve:** www.divorce.co.uk

⇨ **NatCen:** www.natcen.ac.uk

⇨ **NSPCC:** www.nspcc.org.uk

⇨ **Office for National Statistics:** www.statistics.gov.uk

⇨ **One Parent Families | Gingerbread:** www.oneparentfamilies.org.uk

⇨ **One Plus One:** www.oneplusone.org.uk

⇨ **Relate:** www.relate.org.uk

⇨ **Resolution:** www.resolution.org.uk

⇨ **Seddons:** www.seddons.co.uk

⇨ **YouGov:** www.yougov.com

ACKNOWLEDGEMENTS

The publisher is grateful for permission to reproduce the following material.

While every care has been taken to trace and acknowledge copyright, the publisher tenders its apology for any accidental infringement or where copyright has proved untraceable. The publisher would be pleased to come to a suitable arrangement in any such case with the rightful owner.

Chapter One: Marriage Trends

Changing marriage, © One Plus One, *Marriage, relationships and family trends*, © Family and Parenting Institute, *Marriage rates fall to lowest on record*, © Crown copyright is reproduced with the permission of Her Majesty's Stationery Office, *Cohabitees aspire towards marriage*, © London School of Economics and Political Science, *Marriage survey results*, © Seddons, *Is it the beginning of the end for marriage?*, © Guardian Newspapers Limited, *The 'common-law marriage' myth*, © NatCen, *Why adultery can help save a marriage*, © Guardian Newspapers Limited, *Cohabitation*, © Resolution, *The changing family*, © London School of Economics and Political Science, *Love by numbers*, © Guardian Newspapers Limited, *What is a forced marriage?*, © Crown copyright is reproduced with the permission of Her Majesty's Stationery Office, *Escaping forced marriage*, © Crown copyright is reproduced with the permission of Her Majesty's Stationery Office, *'Thousands' of British girls in forced marriages*, © Telegraph Group Limited.

Chapter Two: Divorce and Separation

Divorce and dissolution of civil partnership, © Resolution, *The end of a marriage*, © Care for the Family, *Divorces*, © Crown copyright is reproduced with the permission of Her Majesty's Stationery Office, *Legal jargon explained*,

© Mills and Reeve, *Risk of divorce*, © Divorce Online, *45 per cent of marriages will end in divorce*, © Crown copyright is reproduced with the permission of Her Majesty's Stationery Office, *Caught in the crossfire*, © Relate, *Kids in the middle*, © Fatherhood Institute, *The emotional cost of parental separation*, © Centre for Separated Families, *Happiness, hopes and wellbeing*, © Centre for Separated Families, *Divorce law and your children*, © Divorce Aid, *Contact patterns after separation and divorce*, © One Parent Families | Gingerbread, *Mediation and you*, © Divorce Online.

Photographs
Flickr: page 18 (Meghan Doyle).
Stock Xchng: pages 5 (Randa Clay); 7 (Olly Bennett); 10 (Andrew C.); 11 (Simon Cataudo); 14 (Sanja Gjenero); 23 (Omar Franco); 26 (Steve Woods); 27, 38 (Lynne Lancaster); 31 (Ned Horton).

Illustrations
Pages 1, 13, 20, 34: Don Hatcher; pages 4, 17: Bev Aisbett; pages 6, 19, 28, 37: Angelo Madrid; pages 8, 12, 16, 29: Simon Kneebone.

Additional editorial by Claire Owen, on behalf of Independence Educational Publishers.

And with thanks to the team: Mary Chapman, Sandra Dennis, Claire Owen and Jan Sunderland.

Lisa Firth
Cambridge
January, 2009